A

TREATISE

ON

ATONEMENT

❖

A TREATISE ON ATONEMENT

In which the finite nature of sin is argued;
Its cause and consequences as such;
The necessity and nature of atonement;

And its glorious consequences in the
final reconciliation of all people
to holiness and happiness.

Hosea Ballou
author of *Notes on the Parables
of the New Testament* (1804)

❖

Edited by Dan Harper

San Mateo, California
Fish Island Books, 2015

A Treatise on Atonement by Hosea Ballou
Edited by Dan Harper
Copyright © 2015 Dan Harper.
All rights reserved.

Ballou, Hosea.
       A treatise on atonement.
       220 p.   23 cm.
       Ed. Dan Harper.

ISBN: 978-0-9889413-4-2

Fish Island Books
books.fishisland.net

Contents

Preface to the 2015 Edition vii
A Letter to the Reader 1
The Author's Preface to the Fifth (1832) Edition 11

Part One: Of Sin

1. Its Nature 15
2. Its Origin 23
3. Its Consequences 45

Part Two: Atonement for Sin

4. Erroneous Theories of Atonement 63
5. The Necessity of Atonement, and Where Satisfaction Must Be Made 90
6. The Personage and Character of the Mediator 100
7. Atonement in Its Nature 107

Part Three: Consequences of Atonement to Mankind

8. Salvation Must Be Universal 121
9. The Most Frequent Objections Answered 129
10. Reasons for Believing in Universal Reconciliation 158

Appendix: Biography of Hosea Ballou 205
Scripture Index 211
General Index 217

Preface to the 2015 Edition

Why print a twenty-first century edition of an early nineteenth century book about universal salvation?

Because there are still a great many people who profess the self-contradictory belief in a loving God who tortures too many human beings by condemning them to eternal damnation. *A Treatise on Atonement*, first published in 1805, argues with these people on their own ground, using extensive scriptural references, and proves conclusively that such beliefs are not only incorrect, but destructive of morality, happiness, and holiness.

Hosea Ballou, the author of *A Treatise on Atonement*, doesn't want to push his readers to believe anything unbelievable. He is sure that anyone who is willing to listen to reason, anyone who will read the Bible with an open mind, will be convinced of the truth of universal salvation: that God is love, and that God's love will lead to universal holiness and happiness for all persons.

Ballou's arguments are effective in part because he writes in plain language that is filled with solid common sense. He uses down-to-earth stories and everyday logic as he proves that a loving God would not condemn a part of the human race to eternal punishment. He may not be as polished as today's university professors who write about religion, but he is easier to understand. When you read his book, you feel as though you're having a conversation with a friendly companion. You can relax with him, and he gives you time to think through difficult religious questions.

Ballou wants you to be convinced of the truth of universal salvation because he knows that this truth will "happify" you. That's his common sense term for it: you will be "happified." Ballou knows that belief in hell and eternal damnation makes people unhappy—unhappy for no reason, for belief in hell and damnation is false belief. Once we accept the truth that God is love, says Ballou, "the cause of truth wants nothing in its service but the fruits of the Spirit, which are love, joy, peace, gentleness, goodness, faith, meekness, and temperance" (p. 200).

This new edition of *A Treatise on Atonement* is designed to make Ballou's book accessible to today's readers. Ballou' original paragraphs extended across one or two pages; we are no longer accustomed to such a style. I found those long paragraphs could easily be divided into shorter paragraphs, making them much easier to read. In addition, I added section breaks showing logical divisions within chapters. Like any good preacher, Ballou knows that sometimes people's minds will wander, and he provides re-entry points, places where he makes it easy for you to rejoin the flow of his argument. The section breaks show those re-entry points, those logical divisions in his argument. If you find yourself losing the thread of the argument, simply jump forward to the next section, and start reading there.

This edition includes other aids to the reader. For those who would like to know more about Ballou, an appendix has a brief biography written towards the end of his life. For readers who want to follow Ballou's scriptural arguments more easily, I have inserted scriptural references, and appended a scripture index. A general index includes references to persons, places, and theological topics; I have also indexed Ballou's vivid illustrations and parables. All these things should make it easier for you to read and enjoy this delightful book.

I admit that sometimes *A Treatise on Atonement* can be difficult for today's readers to follow. Ballou wrote in the style of the late eighteenth century, a style with which we are no longer familiar. And, as Ballou himself admitted in his preface to the 1832 edition, he was not the best of writers. But Ballou was an excellent *preacher*, and I find that when I come to a difficult passage in *A Treatise on Atonement*, I can always make sense out of it if I read it out loud. Or if I imagine I am sitting in a comfortable old wooden church, and Ballou is *preaching* to me, then I find him easier to understand.

I also find it helps if you approach this book as a collection of shorter arguments, each of which can be read separately. Each chapter can be taken on its own; each section within a chapter represents a coherent argument which can be read on its own. You can dip into the book at random, stopping when one of his stories, illustrations, or arguments attracts you.

There are places where Ballou sounds dated. His attitudes towards Jews, for example, are simply incorrect, and contradict his central point that all persons are equally worthy of God's love. Then too, he lived before the great flood of research into the Bible and the early history of Christianity—research which we now take for granted—so he may seem to miss the point of some Biblical texts. And, like everyone in his day and age, he refers to humanity with the gender-specific words "man" and "mankind." I suggest you read this book critically, but with an open mind. Ballou, in his Preface to the 1832 edition, tells how he changed his views over his lifetime; if her were alive today, I have no doubt that he would correct some of what he wrote in 1805. Read critically, but remember that with all its flaws, the central point of *A Treatise on Atonement* remains true: a loving God could never tolerate eternal damnation.

A note on the text:

I have silently changed punctuation and paragraphing to make the text easier to read. I made a very few editorial changes to make the text more readable (e.g., changing the old-fashioned word "graffed" to "grafted"). The few footnotes are mine.

This edition draws primarily from the text of the 1832 edition, which represents Ballou's final rewriting of the book. However, as A. A. Miner did in the 1882 edition, I have generally removed the authorial "we" of the 1832 edition in favor of the more personal "I" of earlier editions. I have retained Miner's chapter divisions— divisions that were really inherent in Ballou's text—but I have taken the titles for the chapters more directly from Ballou's descriptions of the divisions of his book.

I have indented many of the quotations from the Bible to make it easier to follow Ballou's arguments from scripture. I have supplied many Bible citations that Ballou omitted. Ballou often misquoted the Bible slightly—no doubt he wrote down many of these passages from memory—but I have generally not corrected his misquotations, although occasionally I have added ellipses to show when he left words out of a particular quotation.

I have included both a scripture index to allow the reader to track down specific Bible references, and a general index for other references.

Acknowledgements

Portions of this book originally appeared on my Web site in 2005, the bicentennial of the *Treatise's* publication. Thanks to Steven Rowe of South Carolina, Rev. Scott Wells of Washington, D.C., and Russell Allen of Australia for their help with the Web version. Scott provided additional encouragement and information.

Thanks to the congregations I served while working on this project: the Unitarian Universalist Society of Geneva, Illinois; First Unitarian Church of New Bedford, Massachusetts; and the Unitarian Universalist Church of Palo Alto, California. The New Bedford church had to put up with a lot of sermons on Universalism, and I thank them for their perceptive comments and their patience.

Finally, thanks to Carol Steinfeld for all her support.

—Dan Harper, San Mateo, Calif., 2015

A

TREATISE

ON

ATONEMENT

TREATISE ON ATONEMENT

A Letter to the Reader

CHRISTIAN READER,—

I know it is frequently the case, when a person takes a new work in hand, he first casts his eye over the title page; and if he find no word on it that indicates perverse sentiments, and the name or denomination of the author he finds agreeable, he may think of having patience to read it; but, being something in a hurry, passes slightly over the preface, supposing it to be of little consequence. But what sensations may have struck your mind on reading the title of this book, and finding it to be the intention of the author to prove the doctrine of *universal holiness* and *happiness* through the mediation and power of atoning grace, I cannot say; however, I would invite you to read with candor and attention, not only this letter, but the whole of the work, and make your judgment afterwards.

Many circumstances might be mentioned which in their association have induced me to write and publish the following treatise; but I can say with propriety that the central object was that in which I always find the most happiness, viz. to do what I find most necessary in order to render myself most useful to mankind.

I have from my early youth been much in the habit of inquiring into the things of religion and religious sentiments; and have, for a number of years, seen, or thought I saw, great inconsistencies in what has for a long time passed for orthodoxy in divinity.

The ideas that sin is infinite, and that it deserves an infinite punishment; that the law transgressed is infinite, and inflicts an infinite penalty; and that the great Jehovah took on himself a natural body of flesh and blood, and actually suffered death on a cross to satisfy his infinite justice and thereby save his creatures from endless misery, are ideas which appear to me to be unfounded in the nature of reason and unsupported by divine revelation.

Such notions have, in my opinion, served to darken the human understanding and obscure the Gospel of eternal life; and have rendered what I esteem as divine revelation a subject of discredit to thousands who, I believe, would never have condemned the scriptures had it not been for those gross absurdities being contended for, and the scriptures forced to bend to such significations. Christian authors and preachers have labored much to dissuade those whom they have caused to disbelieve the Christian religion from their infidelity. But in this case, the salt has lost its savor, become good for nothing, and is trodden under foot of men who are too sensible to believe the unreasonable dogmas imposed on the world, either through error or design, and sanctioned by tradition; and too inattentive to search the scriptures faithfully and impartially whereby they might have learned that those errors were neither in them, nor supported by them.

One particular object, therefore, in this work is, if possible, to free the scripture doctrine of atonement from those encumbrances which have done it so much injury; and open a door at least for the subject to be investigated on reasonable grounds, and by fair argument. If we admit that our Creator made us reasonable beings, we ought, of course, to believe that all the truth which is necessary for our belief is not only reasonable, but reducible to our understandings.

In order to come at the subject of atonement, so as have light continually shining along the path which I intend to occupy, I found it necessary to show my reasons for not admitting the doctrine on the ground on which it is usually argued: to do which I found I must, of necessity, show that the common notion of the infinity of sin is unfounded in truth; and of course, every consequence deducible from such an error, equally unfounded and unsupported. It may seem not a little strange to some of my readers that I dispute the infinity of law against which sin is committed; as all unholiness must be either in union or disunion with the eternal law of holiness and divine purity. But if the reader will take a little pains to observe particularly, it will appear plain that no being can stand amenable to a law above his capacity. And as the creature is finite in his earthly character, in which character only he is or can be a sinner, it is not reasonable to say that he stands amenable to an infinite law. But as the reader will find in this work, so much of the divine law of perfection as the creature obtains a knowledge of (which, in comparison to the whole, is no more than a shadow to a substance), is the law which he violates by his sin. And though we may speak of the sin in ignorance, it can amount to no more than the production of a virtuous intention thwarted by ignorance, or the same principle by which the beasts of the field, the fowls of the air, and the fish of the sea gratify their various inclinations and appetites. And I do not think my reader will wish to have me prove that such sin is not infinite.

In my argument on the cause or origin of sin, I thought it necessary to hint a little on the general idea of the subject, endeavoring to show the want of propriety in what is commonly contended for; and I have sought for the rise of unholy temptations in the constitutions of earthly and finite beings. I have endeavored also to trace the causes and consequences of sin (as sin) so as to determine the finite nature of all which belongs to sin as cause and consequence. In any sense in which it can be said that God is the author of any thing whatever, in that sense of speaking it cannot be sin. And in any sense in which any action or event can be said to be endless in its consequences, God must be considered the author of it.

In all the statements which I have made of the doctrinal ideas of others, I have been careful to state no more than what I have read in authors, or heard contended for in preaching, or conversation; and if I have, in any instance, done those ideas any injustice, it was not intended. The reason why I have not quoted any author or spoken of any denomination is, I have not felt it to be my duty nor inclination to write against any name or denomination in the world; but my object has been, what I pray it ever may be, to contend against error wherever I find it; and to receive truth, and support it, let it come from what quarter it may.

For the sake of ease, however, in writing, I reasoned with my opponent, opposer, or objector, meaning no one in particular, but any one who uses the arguments and states the objections which I have endeavored to answer. It is very probable that some may think me too ironical, and in many instances too severe, on what I call error. But I find it very difficult to expose error so as to be understood by all, without carrying, in many instances, my arguments in such a form as may not be agreeable to those who believe in what I wish to correct. I confess I should have been glad to have written on all my inquiries so as not to have displeased any, but to have pleased all, could I have done it and accomplished my main design; but this I was persuaded would be difficult. I have, therefore, paid particular attention to nothing but my main object; depending on the goodness of my reader to pardon what may be disagreeable, in manner or form, as inadvertencies.

What I have written on the subject of the Trinity is mainly to show the reader in what light I view the Mediator, that my general ideas of atonement may be the easier understood. And though I think my objections and arguments against the common idea of three distinct persons in the Godhead, who are equal in power and glory, to be unanswerable; yet it was not my intention to attend to a full refutation of those ideas, as I think that has frequently been done, and well done.

The opposers of Universalism have generally written and contended against the doctrine under an entire mistaken notion of it. They have endeavored to show the absurdity of believing that men could be received into the kingdom of glory and righteousness in their sins; which no Universalist ever believed. In this work, I have endeavored to make as fair a statement of what I call

Universalism as I was able; and it stands on such ground, that the propriety of it can no more be disputed than the propriety of universal holiness and reconciliation to God. Perhaps the reader will say he has read a number of authors on the doctrine of universalism and finds considerable difference in their systems. That I acknowledge is true; but all agree in the main point, viz. that *universal holiness and happiness* is the *great object of the gospel plan*.

And as for the different ways in which individuals may believe this work will be done, it proves nothing against the main point; but proves what I wish could be proved concerning all other Christian denominations, that they have set up no standard of their own to cause all to bow to, or be rejected as heretics. We feel our own imperfections; we wish for every one to seek with all his might after wisdom; and let it be found where it may, or by whom it may, we humbly wish to have it brought to light, that all may enjoy it; but do not feel authorized to condemn an honest inquirer after truth for what he believes different from a majority of us.

A few sentences which the reader will find towards the close of this work, which have reference to a punishment after death, may cause him to desire more of my ideas on the subject.

The doctrine of punishment after death has, by many able writers, been contended for; some of whom have argued such punishment to be endless, and others limited. But it appears to me that they have taken wrong ground who have endeavored to support the latter, as well as those who have labored to prove the former. They have both put great dependence on certain figurative and parabolical expressions, or passages of scripture, which they explain so as to cause them to allude to such an event. It appears to me that they have not sufficiently attended to the nature of sin so as to learn its punishment to be produced from a law of necessity and not a law of penalty.

Had they seen this, they would also have seen that a perpetuity of punishment must be connected with an equal continuance of sin, on the same principle that an effect is dependent on its cause. Who in the world would contend that a man who had sinned one year could expiate his guilt by sinning five more, with greater turpitude of heart? State the punishment, say a thousand years, for a sinner who dies in unbelief. What is it for? Say for his incorrigibleness in this world. Well, does he commit sin during these thousand years? Surely, or he could not be miserable. Then I ask, if it take a thousand years punishment in another world, to reward the sinner for, say, fifty years of sin in this, how long must he be punished afterwards for the sin he commits during the thousand years? The punishment, or sufferings, which we endure in consequence of sin is not a dispensation of any penal law, but of the law of necessity, in which law as long as a cause continues, it produces its effects. Therefore, to prove a man will suffer condemnation for sin at thirty, forty, or fifty years of age, it would be necessary to prove that he would be a sinner at that time, or those times. So, in order to prove that a man will be miserable after this mortal life is ended, it must first be proved that he will sin in the next state of existence.

It has been argued by many that the doctrine of future punishment or misery is a necessary doctrine to dissuade men from committing sin, which surely surprises me. To tell a person who is in love of sin that if he does not immediately refrain, he will have to continue in sin for a long time, would be true, besure; but would be void of force to dissuade him from what he is in love with. I believe that as long as men sin, they will be miserable, be that time longer or shorter; and that as soon as they cease from sin, they begin to experience divine enjoyment.

The scripture speaks of the times of the restitution of all things, but does not inform us their number, or their duration. It also speaks of the fullness of times, but gives us no date, or duration of them.

I have not stated so many objections against the doctrine

which I have labored to prove, as many of my readers may wish I had, nor so many as I should have been glad to, was it not for swelling the work to more of an expensive size. But I have stated and endeavored to answer the most frequent objections, and those on which my opposers put the most dependence; and I should have taken great satisfaction in communicating many more arguments, both from reason and scripture, in favor of universal holiness and happiness than I have, was it not for the reason assigned in the other case. However, if those objections which I have taken notice of are answered to the reader's satisfaction, other scriptures generally used as argument against the salvation of all men will not be hard to be understood as not unfavorable to the doctrine. And as for the proofs which I have deduced from scripture and reason, I believe them entirely conclusive: but if not, more of the same kind would not be.

The reason I have not particularly explained those parables of the New Testament which I have had occasion to notice in this work is that my *Notes*,* of which mention is made on the title page of this book, are before the public, and contain my ideas on most of the parables spoken by Christ.

A question may be asked by many, which has labored much in my mind, respecting the propriety of publishing books on Divinity, when we profess to believe in the book called the Bible, that it contains all which we mean to communicate as truth in matters of religion; on which question I am determined for myself that the Gospel of Jesus Christ would have been better understood had the Bible been the only book ever read on the subject. And though I doubt not but many authors have done great justice to those subjects on which they have written, and the light of the scriptures have, by such means, been caused to shine; yet, by others, it has been greatly obscured. And had one half the attention been paid to the Bible which has been paid to those authors who

---

* Ballou's *Notes on the Parables of the New Testament* (1804). —Editor.

have written upon it, it would, in my opinion, have been incomparably better for Christendom. But on account of errors imbibed, in consequence of erroneous annotations, it may be argued that it is now necessary to write and publish correct sentiments by the same parity of reasoning as we argue the necessity of those means to restore health, which are not necessary to continue it.

To the short exhortation with which the believer in Universalism will meet in this work, he is humbly invited to pay strict attention; as no faith, however true it may be, can be of any real service to the believer unless it be accompanied with the spirit and life of that truth in which it is grounded. The greater the beauty of a person, the more lamentable his death. The more divinity there is in any faith, the greater is the pity it should not be alive. "As the body without the spirit is dead, so faith without works is dead also." (James ii. 26.)

My brethren in the ministry will not think it assuming that I have spoken of the necessity of our paying strict attention to the stewardship into which God by his grace hath put us; as it was not written so much to instruct, as to show the brethren my faith that they may see the ground on which I land; know the manner in which I contend for the faith once delivered to the saints; and feel for me the same fellowship which I feel for them. You may regret that my ideas were not more correct, in many instances, and think the great subject on which I have written might have obtained better justice from some more experienced writer; in which you have the same ideas with myself.

But in this you may be satisfied, that I have written as I now think and believe, without leaning to the right, or to the left, to please or displease. I have been often solicited to write and publish my general ideas on the gospel, but have commonly observed to my friends that it might be attended with disagreeable consequences, as it is impossible to determine whether the ideas which we entertain at the present time are agreeable to those which we shall be under the necessity of adopting after we have had more experience; and knowing to my satisfaction that authors are very liable to feel such an attachment to sentiments which they have openly avowed to the world that their prejudice frequently obstructs their further acquisitions in the knowledge of the truth; and even in cases of conviction, their own self-importance will keep them from acknowledging their mistakes. And having some knowledge of my own infirmities, I felt the necessity of precaution, which I have no reason to believe is, or has been, injurious.

It has often been said by the enemies of the doctrine for which I have contended, that it would do to live by, but not to die by; meaning that it would not give the mind satisfaction when sensible it was about to leave a mortal for an immortal state. As to the truth of the assertion, I cannot positively say; that moment has not yet been experience by me; and as those who make the remark have never believed the doctrine, I cannot see how they should know any better than I do.

This much I can say: I believe I have seen and often heard of persons rejoicing in the doctrine in the last hours of their lives; but I do not build my faith on such grounds. The sorrows or the joys of persons in their last moments, prove nothing to me of the truth of their general belief. A Jew, who despises the name of Christ from the force of his education, may be filled with comfortable hopes in his last moments, from the force of the same education. I have no doubt but a person may believe, or pretend to believe, in the doctrine of universal salvation when he knows of no solid reason for his belief, but has rather rested the matter on the judgment of those in whom he has placed more confidence than he has in reality on the Savior of the world; and I think it very possible that such Universalists may have strange and unexpected fears when the near approach of death, or any other circumstance, should cause them to think more seriously on so weighty a subject.

What my feelings might be, concerning the doctrine which I

believe, was I called to contemplate it on a death-bed, I am as unable to say as I am what I may think of it a year hence should I live and be in health. But I am satisfied, beyond a doubt, that if I live a year longer, and then find cause to give up my present belief, that I shall not feel a consciousness of having professed what I did not sincerely believe; and was I called to leave the world and my writings in it, and at the last hour of my life should find I had erred, yet I am satisfied that I should possess the approbation of a good conscience in all I have written.

Therefore, though sensible of my imperfections, yet enjoying great consolation in believing the doctrine for which I have argued in the following work, and in the enjoyment of a good conscience, I submit the following pages to a generous and candid public, praying for the blessing of the God whom I serve on the feeble endeavors of the most unworthy whom he hath called as a servant of all men.

—THE AUTHOR

The Author's Preface to the Fifth (1832) Edition

As this edition of the treatise on atonement in several respects varies from former editions, the author feels that he owes it to the public to offer some reason for such variations.

It has pleased God to continue his life until this work has passed through four editions, with all the imperfections which it contained when first published nearly thirty years ago. For a number of years, he has seen reasons to doubt the correctness of some of the opinions which he entertained at the time he wrote the work; and also the propriety of the use he then made of certain passages of scripture.

In his preface to the first edition, he says; "I have had, for sometime, an intention to write a treatise on this subject, but thought of deferring it until more experience might enable me to perform it better, and leisure give me opportunity to be more particular. But the consideration of the uncertainty of life was one great stimulus to my undertaking it at this time, added to a possibility of living to be informed with what success it meets in the world, and of having an opportunity to correct whatever I might, in my future studies, find incorrect, were not the smallest causes of my undertaking it." Now as he has lived to know that the denomination of Christians to which he belongs, has given to this humble work a much more favorable reception than he had any reason to anticipate, and bestowed on it an attention which far exceeds his most flattering hopes; and as he has, as he thinks, improved in his understanding in certain particulars, so as to feel satisfied that the work needed correction; he felt bound, in duty to himself and the public, to make such corrections as his present views required.

But be it known, and duly considered, that in no particular has the author's views undergone any change unfavorable to the main doctrine, to the support of which the treatise was devoted.

The main points in relation to which his views now differ from those he entertained when he first wrote the following work, relate to the pre-existence of Christ; of man's existence before his corporeal organization; and the application of some passages of scripture solely to the purifying operations of divine truth in man's understanding, which passages he now believes embraced, in their true sense, all the temporal judgments with which a most perverse and wicked generation was visited.

Although he then as fully believed in the dependence of Christ on his God and Father as he now does, he entertained the opinion that he had a sentinent existence before he was manifested in flesh; and he then thought that certain passages of scripture evidently supported that opinion. These passages, though they seem to favor such a sentiment, do not appear altogether sufficient fully to warrant the belief of it. Could the opinion now be fully supported that Christ existed in a sentinent state before he was manifested in the flesh, it would not be difficult to yield to a belief that Adam also had an existence before he was formed of the dust of the ground. However these things are in fact, they now appear to the author as points of mere speculation, much too obscure to be laid down as matters of faith.

It is of importance here to remark that the moral relation which the treatise originally represented man to hold to the Creator, from which relation momentous deductions were drawn, is still believed; and all those deductions are retained.

To the foregoing it may be proper to add that the doctrine of a future disciplinary state, and the application of certain passages of scripture to that state of suffering which were left in suspense, undecided, in the treatise originally, were so left on account of the author's mind being then undecided in relation to these subjects. He was, however, as well convinced then as now that the doctrine of a future retribution could be supported on no other hypothesis than that of the continuance of sin in a future state; but he was not then so fully satisfied that all which the scriptures say about sin, and the punishment of it, relates solely to this mortal state as he now is.

The author entertains no doubt that many will regret that as an opportunity has offered, the treatise should not be more improved as to its style. As an apology for this defect, he offers two suggestions:— First: He could not consent so entirely to alter the work as to endanger the loss of what has probably given its arguments and easy access to the understanding of common readers. And second: A consciousness that any effort or labor in his power to make or bestow, would, after all, leave many offences to the delicate nice reader.

The author is not willing to neglect this opportunity to tender his grateful acknowledgements to his numerous friends who have so indulgently regarded his different publications, and so extensively patronized his labors. That a growth in the knowledge of divine truth, and treasures laid up where neither moth nor rust can corrupt, may be their recompense, is the sincere prayer of their devoted servant,

—THE AUTHOR.

PART ONE: OF SIN.

In the *Treatise on Atonement*, I shall confine myself to three general inquiries: First: Of Sin. Second: Of Atonement for Sin. Third: Of the Consequences of Atonement to Mankind. These particulars may be represented by a disorder; the remedy for the disorder; and the health enjoyed in consequence of the cure.

And first: Of Sin, which for the sake of ease I subdivide as follows: 1. Its nature; 2. Its cause; 3. Its effects.

1. Of Sin — Its Nature

Sin is the violation of a law which exists in the mind, which law is the imperfect knowledge men have of moral good. This law is transgressed whenever, by the influence of temptation, a good understanding yields to a contrary choice. Where a law exists, it presupposes a legislature whose intention in legislation must be thwarted in order for the law to take cognizance of sin. This legislature, in all moral accountable beings, is a capacity to understand, connected with the causes and means of knowledge, which standing or existing on finite and limited principles will justify my supposition that sin in its nature ought to be considered finite and limited, rather than infinite and unlimited, as has by many been supposed.

By offering my reasons against the infinity of sin, I shall open to an easy method of showing it to be finite. The supposition that sin is infinite is supported, or rather pretended to be supported, on the consideration of its being committed against an infinite law, which is produced by an infinite legislature, who is God himself. I have before observed, and I think justly, that the intention of a legislature in legislation must be thwarted in order for the law to take cognizance of sin.

Now if God, in a direct sense of speaking, be the legislator of the law which is thwarted by transgression, in the same direct sense of speaking, his intentions in legislation are thwarted. With eyes open, the reader cannot but see that if sin be infinite because it is committed against an infinite law whose author is God, the design of Deity must be abortive; to suppose which brings a cloud of darkness over the mind as intense as the supposition is erroneous. It cannot with any propriety be supposed that any rational being can have an intention contrary to the knowledge which he possesses. Was a resolve brought into the State Legislature to be passed into an act, it would be very unlikely to succeed, providing the legislature knew that the intention of the act would utterly fail. It is possible, and very frequently the case, that imperfect beings desire contrary to their knowledge; but this in every instance is proof and often the cause of their misery. In such cases, misery rises to an exact proportion to the strength of desire.

Now to reason justly, we must conclude that if God possesses infinite wisdom, he could never intend any thing to take place, or be, that will not take place, or be; nor that which is, or will be, not to be, at the time when it is. And it must be considered erroneous to suppose that the All-wise ever desired any thing to take place, which by his prescience, he knew would not; as such a supposition must in effect suppose a degree of misery in the Eternal Mind equal to the strength of his fruitless desire! Were this the case, all the misery to which mortals are subject bears not the thousandth part of the proportion to the miseries of the Divine Being, as the smallest imaginable atom does to the weight of the ponderous globe; providing, at the same time, the idea of infinity is attached to Deity!

Again, if we admit of a disappointment to the Supreme Being even in the smallest matter, it follows that we have no satisfactory evidence whereby to prove that any thing, at present, in the whole universe is as He intended. All the harmonies of nature, which to the eye of wondering man are so convincing of the existence of that power, wisdom, and goodness which he adores, may have continued their laws in active force much longer than God intended; brought into existence millions of beings more than were contemplated in creation; and by this time become a perfect nuisance to the general plan of the Almighty. The admission of the error refuted would sink the mind to the nether parts of moral depravity, where darkness reigns with all its horrors.

The above arguments are introduced to show the absurdity of admitting a violation of the intention of the Supreme Legislator.

I now turn on the other side, and admit as a fact what I have sufficiently refuted, viz. that the intentions of God as a Supreme Legislator are violated by the sin of finite beings; but must beg leave to inform the reader that the proposition will by no means afford the intended consequences; but yields me an argument in favor of the finite nature of sin, which I do not want, and of which I shall make no other use than to explode the proposition itself. If any intention of Deity were ever thwarted, it proves without evasion that he is not infinite; if so, his will, or intention, cannot be infinite; and therefore the consequences intended by the proposition are forever lost, as they exist only upon the supposition of his being infinite. If it be argued that the intentions of Deity as a legislator are violated, not strictly in an infinite sense but in some subordinate degree, it is giving up the ground contended for, to all intents; for if the intention violated be not infinite, the sin of violating it cannot be infinite.

Again, if sin be infinite and unlimited, it cannot be superseded by any principle or being in the universe; for goodness cannot be more than infinite, neither is there a degree for Deity to occupy above it. And it may be further argued that the admission of the error refuted would be a denial of any Supreme Being in the universe; for, as Deity does not supersede sin, he cannot be superior to that which is equal to himself.

Again, I further inquire, can that be considered as an infinite evil which is limited in its consequences? The answer must be in the negative. If sin be an infinite evil, and infinite in its consequences as an evil, not only all created beings must suffer endlessly by it, but God himself can never cease to experience the torment-giving power of that which he is unable to avoid; I say more, if sin is infinite and unlimited (for it must be unlimited if it be infinite), it follows that there is no such principle in the universe as any one property which we are wont to attribute to the Almighty: for, if once we admit a principle of divine justice to have an existence, it is granted that sin is bounded by it and therefore cannot be infinite; and it is a fact that sin can nowhere exist, only where it can be compared with justice. Again, it ought not to be supposed that the intentions of Deity were ever violated, if we admit at the same time that he had power to avoid such violation. And who, in their senses, will say that that which is unavoidable by God, is avoidable by man?

Enough, undoubtedly, is said to show the egregious mistake of supposing sin to be infinite; and more need not be written on the subject were it not by some contended that Job xxii. 5 is in full proof of the infinity of sin. "Is not thy wickedness great? and thine iniquities infinite?" In answer to this passage, I need only turn the reader to chap. xlii. 7:

> And it was so, that after the Lord had spoken these words unto Job, the Lord said unto Eliphaz the Timanite, my wrath is kindled against thee, and against thy two friends, for ye have not spoken of me the thing that is right, as my servant Job hath.

Observe, kind reader, the words which are brought to prove the infinity of sin are neither the words of God nor of one whom he approved; but they are the words of that Timanite against whom God's anger was kindled, for not speaking the thing that was right.

Once more, and I close this part of my query:— If sin be infinite in its nature, there can be no one sin greater than another. The smallest offence against the good of society is equal to blasphemy against the Holy Ghost. If what we call a small crime be not infinite, the greatest cannot be, providing there is any proportion between the great and the small. Are not the words of Christ, Matt. xii. 31, where he speaks of sins and blasphemies that should be forgiven unto men, and of blasphemies that should not be forgiven men, a sufficient evidence that some sins are more heinous than others? Again, 1st Epistle of John v. 16, where some sins are said to be not unto death, and some unto death, etc.

Now, admitting the matter proved, that sin is not infinite, it follows, of course, that it is proved to be finite. However, we will now attend to the direct evidences of the finite nature of sin.

The law which takes cognizance of sin is not infinite, not in the sense in which it is violated, it being produced by the legislature which I have before noticed, viz. a capacity to understand, connected with the causes and means of knowledge. In order for a law to be infinite, the legislature must be so; but man's ability to understand is finite and all the means which are in his power for the acquisition of knowledge are finite; all his knowledge is circumscribed, and the law produced by such causes must be like them, not infinite but finite. An infinite law would be far above the capacity of a finite being, and it would be unreasonable to suppose man amenable to a law above his capacity. All our knowledge of good and evil is obtained by comparison. We call an action "evil" by comparing it with one which we call "good." Were it in our power to embrace all the consequences that are connected with our actions in our intentions, our meanings would seldom be what they now are.

Had it been so with the brethren of Joseph when they sold him to the Ishmaelites, that they then knew all the consequences which would attend the event, they would not have meant it, as they did, for evil; but seeing with perfectly unbeclouded eyes their own salvation, and that of the whole family of promise, they would have meant it for good, as did the Almighty who superintended the affair. Now the act of selling Joseph was sin, in the meaning of those who sold him; but it was finite, considered as sin, for it was bounded by the narrowness of their understandings, limited by their ignorance, and circumscribed by the wisdom and goodness of him who meant it for good. If this sin had been infinite, nothing we can justly call good, could have been the consequence; but whoever can read the event without seeing that the best of consequences were connected with it?

The promised seed in whom all the families of the earth are to be blessed, according to the word of promise to Abraham, was to descend from that family which was preserved through seven years of famine, as a consequence of the good intended in that event. And who but God can comprehend the infinite good contained in all the glorious plan of mediatorial grace? We then see that what in a limited sense we may justly call sin, or evil, in an unlimited sense is justly called good.

We say of the top of yonder mountain it is exceedingly high; and of yonder valley, it is low; and this we justly say, by comparing one with the other, in respect to the centre of our earth. But the moment we extend our thoughts to contemplate the millions of worlds in unbounded space, and take the whole in one grand system, the idea of high and low is lost. So is sin finished, when, by divine grace, our understandings are enlightened, and we hear our spiritual Joseph say, "Grieve not yourselves, ye meant it unto evil, but God meant it unto good." (See Gen. xlv. 5.)

It will be granted, on all sides, that no action unconnected with design ought to be considered sin; it is then an evil intention that constitutes an evil action. For instance, a man exerting himself to the utmost of his abilities to save the life of his neighbor accidentally takes his life; the consequence is not the guilt of murder, but heart-aching grief for the loss of his friend. Again, a man exerting himself with all his ingenuity and strength to take the life of his neighbor misses his intention and saves his life from immediate danger; the consequence is not the approbation of a good conscience for having saved the life of his neighbor, but condemnation for having designed his death, and perhaps mortification in his disappointment.

By these instances, the reader may see that no act can be determined to be morally good, or evil, by the consequences which follow, but only by the disposition, or intention, which the actor possesses when the act is done. Then in order for the sin to be infinite, the intention of the transgressor must be infinite, embracing all the consequences that can ever arise from what he does; but this is never the case with finite beings. We never know all the effects or consequences that will be produced from the smallest of those acts which we do in time. It is the immediate consequences which we have in our power to calculate upon, and in them we are often deceived. Our acts as moral accountables are all limited to the narrow circle of our understanding; therefore our goodness is limited, being of the finite nature of our knowledge, and our sin is in the same finite and limited circle.

It may be argued very justly that as no finite cause can produce an infinite effect, no finite creature can commit an infinite sin; and as every effect must stand in relation to its cause, so man being finite cannot be the cause of an evil which does not stand in relation to man the finite cause. Should the reader suppose that my admitting the act of selling Joseph was attended with unlimited consequences is in opposition to my sentiment wherein I limit all actions which originate in finite causes; I reply, as the act of selling Joseph respected the purpose of Deity and the plan of grace, those who sold him do not stand as even the shadow of a cause, but only as instruments by which God effected his own divine and gracious purpose.

Perhaps the reader by this time is ready to say, according to this reasoning, there can be no such things as real evil in the universe. If, by real evil, is meant something that ought not to be, in respect to all the consequences which attend it, I cannot admit of its existence; for I cannot conceive of any productive cause whatever, that can be, strictly speaking, limited in its consequences. For instance, the first transgression of man, no one can suppose has ceased in its consequences; for, from that cause, the knowledge of good and evil exists in moral beings, and when the effects of that knowledge will cease, I cannot imagine. If it be objected that to call that a sin which produces an infinite continuance of good effects must be absurd; I say, in reply, the objection comes too late; for it is already proved, that the consequences of an act do not determine whether the act be good or evil.

I have, in the foregoing queries, spoken of that kind of sin which is productive of remorse; however, we read, besure, of the sin of ignorance, see Num. xv. 27, etc.; but this I conceive to be more of a legal than of a moral nature, and it is sometimes called error; it is in a thousand instances productive of sorrow and disappointment, but never of guilt. If we consider the Jews under the law, or the Gentiles, who, the apostle says, were a law unto themselves, we shall find them exposed to guilt on the same principles. Therefore, moral transgression must vary, as the knowledge and understanding of men vary, in various circumstances.

If it be thought by the reader that I have passed over the spirit of the law, which is love to God in a superlative degree, and an esteem for our neighbors equal to that which we have for ourselves (see Matt. xx. 37-39; Luke x. 27); I answer, I have not altogether passed by it. This law of divine love is that infinite law of perfection which is higher than our capacities extend, in a finite state. The law given to Israel, literally speaking, was only a shadow of the spirit of love; and all our knowledge of moral holiness is but a faint resemblance of that sublime rectitude from which the most upright of the sons of men are at a great distance.

Having said so much on the nature of sin as to make the subject plain to the reader's understanding, I will now pass to an inquiry into its cause, or origin.

2. Of Sin — Its Origins

The origin of sin has, among Christians in general, been very easily accounted for; but in a way, I must confess, that never gave me any satisfaction since I came to think for myself on subjects of this nature.

A short chimerical story of the bard, Milton, has given perfect satisfaction to millions respecting the introduction of moral evil into the moral system which we occupy. The substance of the account is that sometime before the creation of man, the Almighty created multitudes of spiritual beings called angels. Some of these creatures of God were much higher in dignity and authority than others, but all perfectly destitute of sin or moral turpitude. One, dignified above all the rest, stood Prime Minister of the Almighty, clothed with the highest missive power, and clad with garments of primeval light; obsequious to nothing but the high behest of his Creator, he discharged the functions of his office with a promptitude and dignity, suited to the eminency of his station, and to the admiration of celestial millions. But when it pleased Jehovah to reveal the brightness of his glory and the image of the Godhead in humanity, he gave forth the command, see Psalm xcvii. 7: "Worship him, all ye Gods." And Heb. i. 6:

And again, when he bringeth the first begotten into the world,
he saith, and let all the angels of God worship him.

Lucifer, Son of the Morning (as Christians have called him), surprised at the idea of worshipping any being but God himself, looked on the Son with ineffable disdain, and in a moment grew indignant, rebelled against God, challenged supremacy with the Almighty, and cast his eye to the sides of the north as a suitable place to establish his empire. Legions of spirits followed this chief in rebellion, and formed a dangerous party in the kingdom of the Almighty. The Son of God was invested with full power as Generalissimo of Heaven, to command the remaining forces against the common enemy. And in short, after many grievous battles between armies of contending spirits, where life could not in the least be exposed, Lucifer and his party were driven out of Heaven, leaving it in peace, though in a great measure depopulated!

God having created the earth and placed the first man and woman in a most happy situation of innocence and moral purity, without the smallest appetite for sin or propensity to evil, the arch Apostate enviously looked from his fiery prison, to which he was consigned by the command of the Almighty, and beholding man placed in so happy a situation, and in a capacity to increase to infinite multitudes by which the kingdom of Heaven would be enlarged, was determined to crop this tree in the bud. —He therefore turns into a serpent, goes to the woman and beguiles her, gets her to eat of a fruit which God had forbidden, by which means he introduced sin into our system.

I have not been particular in this sketch, but it contains the essence of the common idea. I shall now put it under examination, looking diligently for the propriety of accounting for the origin of moral evil in this way.

And first, of this memorable rebellion in heaven! It seems that this rebel angel was always obedient to the commands of his Maker until the hour of his fall; that there was not the least spot of pollution in him until he felt the emotions of pride which lifted him above submission to the Son of God. This being the case, I ask, was this angel ignorant of the real character of the Son, whom he was commanded to worship? If he were not, but knew it to be no other than the true Eternal, his Creator, manifested in a nature which Jehovah created—if he loved his Maker as he ought to do, which none will pretend to dispute—he would have worshiped him with due reverence the moment he made the discovery and heard the command. This no person in his senses will dispute.

If he did not know the real character whom he was commanded to worship, had he complied, he would have worshipped he knew not what. And nothing can be more absurd than to suppose that infinite wisdom would command his creatures to worship ignorantly. I ask further, could purity produce impurity; or moral holiness, unholiness? All answer, no. Was not the angel holy in every faculty? Was not the command, for him to worship the Son, holy and just? All answer, yes. Then from such causes, how was sin produced? The reader will easily see the question cannot be answered.

Now, be so kind as to turn to the scripture to which I have referred on this subject, and see if we have any authority for saying that either gods or angels refused to worship when commanded (Heb. i. 16):

> Again, when he bringeth in the first begotten into the world, he saith, let all the angels of God worship him.

That this first begotten is Christ, no doubt will be entertained. But when was he brought into the world? before, or since, the first transgression of man? Since, most certainly. Then, supposing millions of angels had sinned at that time, it could have had no consequence productive of man's transgression, as a cause cannot be posterior to its effects. Therefore, to suppose that those angels who never sinned until long after man became a transgressor, were the instigators of what is called the fall, discovers a want of calculation.

And further, what authority have we for believing that the command was disobeyed? We find nothing connected with either passage, viz. that in Psalms or that in Hebrews, which intimates a refusal among the gods or angels. And I see no need of supposing that by gods in one text, or by angels in the other, any other beings are intended than men. In respect to the command for all the gods to worship him, I observe, "they were called gods to whom the word of God came, and the scriptures cannot be broken" (John x. 35). And the command for all the angels of God to worship stands on this proper ground; by angels are meant messengers, who are employed by God, for the information of their fellow men; —but as all those messengers, or ministers, were inferior to the "Messenger of the covenant," whom the Lord promised to send unto Jerusalem, it was suitable to show his superiority by giving such a token in the scriptures as commanding all the angels to worship him.

There is another passage in the twenty-fourth of Isaiah, 12, etc.:

> How art thou fallen from Heaven, O Lucifer, Son of the morning! how art thou cut down to the ground, which didst weaken the nations! for thou hast said in thine heart, I will ascend unto heaven; I will exalt my throne above the stars of God; I will sit also upon the mount of the congregation in the sides of the north, etc.

"Here," I have been told, "we have a particular account of the sin which Satan committed in Heaven." But as there is nothing in this passage or its connections that has reference to any other creature or being as Lucifer, Son of the Morning, than the King of Babylon, I shall say but little upon it. Observe, the question is asked, How art thou fallen from heaven, O Lucifer, Son of the Morning? How art thou cut down to the ground, who didst weaken the nations? This Lucifer weakened the nations before he fell, but was unable to weaken them afterwards. He said in his heart he would ascend unto Heaven. Was this the sin of Satan, as is generally supposed? Was he not already in Heaven? How then could he say in his heart, I will ascend unto Heaven? I will not trouble the reader with any thing so vague as the vulgar application of this scripture, only enough to show that it had no such meaning. The King of Babylon is pointed out in this prophecy as exalting his throne above the stars of God, which, in a figurative sense, undoubtedly meant his exalting himself by the reduction of the Jews, who are figuratively called the stars of God.

Again, this angel of light must have been very ignorant of the power and goodness of the Almighty in order to have possessed a thought that to rebel against him could be of any possible advantage, or that he could have carried and maintained a contest with him. If he were as ignorant as all this, the inhabitants of Heaven must have been extremely uncultivated in that age of eternity, and no great ornament to a place so much famed for glory and grandeur. If Heaven, which is said to be God's throne, is or ever was inhabited by defectible beings, the place itself must be a defectible place; and why the Almighty should take up his special abode in a defectible place, surrounded by defectible beings, I cannot imagine. But I pass on.

After Satan was turned out of Heaven, he saw no possible way to injure his adversary, only by contaminating his creatures which he had just made, and placed in the happy situation before described. Here observe the matter appears strange. Did God not know the evil disposition of Satan? Had he forgotten the awful difficulty but just settled? Or would he leave an innocent lamb to the ferocity of a bear robbed of her whelps? God had driven Satan from heaven, from his own presence, but left him at loose ends to prey on his tender offspring, whom he had just left in a defenseless situation on this ball of earth. What would appear more unnatural and shocking than for a father to chase his enemy out at his door, but leave him to slay his defenseless children in the street? I shall, after what I have observed, beg liberty to say that I am so far from believing any such story respecting the cause of sin that I have not even the shadow of evidence, from scripture or reason, to support the sentiment.

But I have been told that man, standing in a state of sinless purity, could not have fallen from that rectitude unless there had been some sinful being to have tempted him. Admitting there is any force in this observation, it stands as directly against the fall of Satan, without a sinful temptation, as it does against man's transgression, without a tempter. Was man more pure before he sinned than that holy angel in Heaven? If not, how could that angel sin without a temptation, more easily than man who was made in a lower grade?

But supposing we should admit that God commanded an angel to worship his Son Jesus, and the angel refused, and call that the first sin ever committed, it would not determine its origin or cause. A cause or origin must exist before an effect or production. So, after all our journeying to heaven after a sinning angel, and after pursuing him to hell, and from hell to the earth, we have not yet answered the question, viz. What is the origin of sin? We have only shown that the way in which this question has been generally solved is without foundation.

Having stated what I have been told was the origin of sin, and given my reasons why I do not believe it, I now come to give my own ideas of the matter.

Scripture, with the assistance of that reason without which the scriptures would be of no more service to us than they are to the brute creation, I shall take for my guide on the question before me. Almighty God is a being of infinite perfection; this the scriptures will support, and reason declare: He was the author of our existence, being the creator of the first man and woman, the occasion of their being formed of the dust of the ground, and the director of that providence by which we are all introduced by ordinary generation. Our maker must have had a design in the works of his hands; this the scriptures argue, and this reason says. The whole of God's design must be carried into effect, and nothing more, admitting him to be an infinite being.

It may assist us in arriving at a satisfactory solution of our subject to consider, in the first place, the origin of natural evil. This is unquestionably the necessary result of the physical organization and constitution of animal nature. In the elements of which our bodies are composed, and in their combination in our constitution, we evidently discover ample provisions for the production of all manner of disorders to which they are incident, and even of mortality itself. A careful examination of our natural senses, as mediums of pleasure and pain and health and sickness, will very naturally lead to a consideration of these same senses as being the origin, as far as we can see, of our thoughts and volitions. With these senses are necessarily connected all the various passions which we possess and which are ever in accordance with the ideas or thoughts by them created. From the ever-changing combinations and various evolutions of these our senses, thoughts, ideas, appetites, and passions are found to originate all that variety of moral character which is found in man.

It has long been the opinion of Christian divines that natural evil owes its origin to what is denominated moral evil or sin, but however respectable this sentiment may be considered on account of the respectability of its advocates, we feel fully convinced that the very reverse of the opinion is true. The doctrine which we feel authorized to reverse contends that natural evil is a judicial infliction on man for his sin, and therefore is the effect of moral evil; but the ground we shall take is that natural evil owes its origin to the original constitution of our animal nature, and that moral evil or sin owes its origin to natural evil.

In order to clearly understand the truth of the position here taken, it is necessary only to notice, with due caution, the origin of our volitions. This, in all cases, is want. If man wanted nothing he would do nothing, nor could he desire to do any thing. Now want unsatisfied is an evil; and unsatisfied want is the first movement to action or volition. The motives which invite to action owe their strength to the nature and strength of desire which want creates, and the moral character of the action depends on the character of the motive.

Thus man, as a partaker of flesh and blood,
was made subject to vanity, not willingly, but by reason of him who subjected the same in hope.

(See Rom. viii. 20.) This hope, which is that sure and steadfast anchor which enters into that within the veil, and expatiates in a life to come, is the title our Creator has given us as heirs of that immortal and eternal life which are brought to light through the Gospel. But from our natural constitution, composed of our bodily elements, we are led to act in obedience to carnal appetites, which justifies the conclusion that sin is the work of the flesh, as expressed by St. Paul in Gal. v. 19-21:

> Now the works of the flesh are manifest, which are these: adultery, fornication, uncleanness, lasciviousness, idolatry, witchcraft, hatred, variance, emulation, wrath, strife, seditions, heresies, envyings, murders, drunkenness, revelings, and such like.

And 1 Cor. iii. 3:

> For ye are yet carnal: for whereas there is among you envying, and strife, and divisions, are ye not carnal and walk as men?

If man had been wholly constituted of flesh and blood, both body and mind, so that he was no more susceptible of moral principles than the beast creation appear to be, then would he never have been capable of committing sin, or of enduring moral evil, any more than do the lower animals around us. We might have had the same natural appetites, desires, and passions which we now have, and might have strove, like all other creatures to gratify them, and might have devoured one another, all without committing sin, or feeling guilt. But we find in man what we may call a law of moral, or spiritual life, of which St. Paul speaks in his epistle to the Romans where he is quite particular in setting forth the contrary workings of the law of the flesh and the law of the spirit of life. Rom. vii. 19-23:

> For the good that I would I do not; but the evil which I would not that I do. Now, if I do that I would not, it is no more I that do it, but sin that dwelleth in me. I find then a law, that, when I would do good, evil is present with me. For I delight in the law of God after the inward man. But I see another law in my members warring against the law of my mind, and bringing me into captivity to the law of sin which is in my members.

And chap. viii. 1-2:

There is, therefore, now no condemnation to them that are in Christ Jesus, who walk not after the flesh, but after the spirit. For the law of the spirit of life in Christ Jesus hath made me free from the law of sin and death.

These conflicting laws of flesh and spirit have always existed in man from his first formation, and so long as they both continue to exert their powers in opposition to each other, so long will sin remain and continue to produce condemnation.

This law of the spirit of life is the spirit of Christ, or the second Adam, of which we read 1 Cor. xv. 45:

> The first man Adam was made a living soul, the last Adam was made a quickening spirit.

This we may say is that image of God in which man was created, as Christ is said to be the "brightness of God's glory, and the express image of his person." (Heb. i. 3.)

By thus accounting for the origin of sin we endeavor to set forth what we believe is the sense of the scripture representation of the subject. James says, chap. i. 14-15:

> But every man is tempted when he is drawn away of his own lust, and enticed. Then when lust hath conceived, it bringeth forth sin; and sin, when it is finished, bringeth forth death.

In the forepart of Genesis, the origin of sin is figuratively represented. There we are informed that man was placed in a garden of delights, to keep it and to dress it. The tree of life was in it, and the tree of the knowledge of good and evil; he was bid welcome to the tree of life, but was forbidden the other. A subtle serpent comes to the woman, and tempts her with the forbidden fruit; she eats, and gives it to her husband, and he also partakes: Their eyes are opened to the knowledge of good and evil; they see that they are naked, and hide themselves from God; sew fig-leaves together for garments to hide their nakedness. God comes into the garden in the cool of the day, calls for the man, and asks him if he had eaten of the forbidden fruit. He answers that the woman whom

God gave him, gave unto him and he ate. The woman is next interrogated, and she lays it to the serpent's guile. The ground is cursed, for Adam's sake; when he tills it, it is to produce briars and thorns; he is to eat his bread by the sweat of his face, and at last return to the dust. The woman's conception was to be multiplied in sorrow, and her desire was to be to her husband, and he was to rule over her. The serpent was cursed above all cattle, was to go on his belly, and to eat dust as long as he lived. This is, in short, the scripture representation of the first sin; and I consider it to be figurative.

Should it be said that this garden was a literal garden, that the tree of life was a literal tree, and that the tree of the knowledge of good and evil was also literal; I should be glad to be informed what evidence can be adduced in support of such an idea. Where is the garden now? Where is the tree of life now? Where is the tree of knowledge of good and evil now? Are those trees now growing on the earth as literal trees? We are not informed, in the scripture, that this garden was carried off to heaven, or that either of those trees was removed. It is written, that God drove the man whom he had made out of the garden, and placed cherubims and a flaming sword at the east of the garden, to prevent the man from approaching the tree of life. If the garden were literal, why could not Adam have gone into it on the north, south, or west side?

The pathway of understanding is now open and clear. God saw fit, in his plan of divine wisdom, to make the creature subject to vanity; to give him a mortal constitution; to fix in his nature those faculties which would, in their operation, oppose the spirit of the heavenly nature. It is therefore said that God put enmity between the seed of the woman, and that of the serpent. And it was by the passions which arose from the fleshy nature that the whole mind became carnal, and man was captivated thereby.

But perhaps the objector will say this denies the liberty of the will, and makes God the author of sin. To which I reply, desiring the reader to recollect what I have said of sin in showing its nature; by which it is discovered that God may be the innocent and holy cause of that which, in a limited sense, is sin; but as it respects the meaning of God, it is intended for good. It is not casting any disagreeable reflections on the Almighty, to say he determined all things for good; and to believe he superintends all the affairs of the universe, not excepting sin, is a million times more to the honor of God than to believe he cannot, or that he does not when he can.

The reader will then ask if God must be considered as the first, the holy, and the innocent cause of sin, is there any unholy or impure causes? I answer, there is, but in a limited sense. There is no divine holiness in any fleshly or carnal exercise; there is no holiness nor purity in all the deceptions ever experienced by imperfect beings; and these are the immediate causes of sin; and as such, they make the best of men on earth groan, and cry out, "Who shall deliver me from the body of this death?" If it should be granted that sin will finally terminate for good in the moral system, it will then be necessary to admit that God is its first cause, or we cannot say that God is the author of all good. If we say that sin is not for the good of God's system but is a damage, we must also say that God would have prevented its taking place if it had been in his power; if it were not in his power, he is not Almighty; neither can we say he is Supreme in an unlimited sense, as he was not superior to the causes which produced sin.

But to say that God is the author of sin, says the reader, sounds very badly, let you put what coloring you please upon it; and if I believed it, I should not dare to say it. Well, what shall I say, in order to please? Say the Devil was the author of sin. But did the Devil make himself? No; God made him an holy angel, and he made himself a devil, by transgression. Well, God made an angel, and that angel made a devil of himself, or any thing else, proves that God was the first cause as directly as any thing which I have argued.

The objector will further say that that angel was made a moral agent, and therefore ought to be considered the author of his own sin. But I say in reply that if God produced an agency, and that agency produced sin, it argues that God is the first cause, and agency the second and effective cause. If this mode of reasoning be faulted, I ask, is not God the origin and cause of all moral righteousness? None can be perverse enough to say no; then I ask, again, If moral agency created by God is not the original cause of moral righteousness, by what rule of reasoning can it be made the original cause of transgression? But I have before refuted the notion about this sinning angel.

I now call the attention of the reader to man, which is our proper study; and attend to the objection as it respects the liberty of the will. But in the first place, for the sake of the argument, I will consent to any liberty of the will which is contended for; and then ask, what was the cause of man's having liberty of will? My opponent must allow it was God. Well, if God produced a liberty of will in man, and that liberty of will produced sin, is there any great difficulty in seeing that that is making God the original cause of sin in every sense in which I have argued it? What would the objector wish to be understood to mean by "will"? If it is anything more or less than choice, I am at a loss about it. If it is choice, then what we have to look into is the liberty of choice.

In order for choice to take place, the mind must have perceptions of two or more objects; and that object which has the most influence on the judgment and passions will be the chosen object; and choice, in this instance, has not even the shadow of liberty. None will be vain enough to say that will, or choice, has any liberty before it exists, and choice does not exist until an object is chosen; and to say choice has liberty to refuse an object after it is chosen is using violence on terms.

And the same will be the conclusion if we take the word will. A person is invited by two friends to make them a visit the same afternoon, at their respective houses; he wishes to visit both, but cannot at the same time. In this circumstance, honored with both their invitations, he feels at a real loss what answer to make; both insist on his compliance with equal earnestness, and with equal influence on his judgment and passions; he still remains without a determination. To end the affair one of his friends says, I will go with you this afternoon and visit our friend, if you and he will return the visit next week. This decides in the mind of him who was first invited, as the other consents to the proposal.

Now, choice, or will, is in favor of visiting, according to the last proposal made. Until the man willed to go, the will to go did not exist; it could have no liberty before it did exist; and after it did, to say that that will which was to go one way was at liberty to go the other, is using the violence before mentioned.

It is then evident, that will, or choice, has no possible liberty. The objector will now move his position and say, It is the mind that has this liberty to choose, or not choose; to will, or not will. In order to determine this matter justly, I first ask, does the power of choosing exist in the mind, or in the object chosen? If it be answered that the power of choice is in the mind, and not in the object which influences the mind, the man who was at a loss to determine which of his friends to visit while the objects were in equal force on his mind was entirely ignorant of it; and admitting it was so, it might as well have been otherwise, for the power of choosing in his mind did him no good; he was, after all, dependent on a certain circumstance, which, being attached to one object made it preferable to the other.

Again, admitting the power of choice to be attributed to the mind, and not to the object which gives perceptions to the mind and influences it, it must be as easy for the mind to choose a minor, as a major object. It will be granted, on all sides, that persons may choose an object in preference to another which is not half so valuable; but this is always in consequence of error in judgment.

Now it is as objects appear to the mind that we ought to consider them in our present query. Supposing a poor man, who has a wife and some hungry children to feed, is offered a dollar or a guinea, for a day's work; he does not know the value of either, not being acquainted with money or its value, or the nature of the metals which are stamped with value. He consults, or means to consult, the good of those for whom he is willing to labor, and would if possible receive that which would do the most towards removing their wants; and says to himself, the dollar is much the largest, and the probability is, it is worth three times as much as the guinea; it is finally his opinion that that is the case.

Now I ask in relation to my argument, which of those pieces of money will he be most likely to choose? The answer is, the dollar. But I ask, why? If his mind is at real liberty, it is no more attached to the dollar than to the guinea; the influence which the dollar has on his mind more than the guinea, destroys not the liberty of the mind to choose the guinea; I wish to be told why he is more likely to choose the dollar than the guinea.

Or, to alter the statement, so that the mind is not deceived. The man perfectly knows the value of both guinea and dollar. The good of his wanting family is what he means to consult; which will he be most likely to choose in this case? answer, the guinea. I ask again, why? Is there any reason, or is there not? There is, and it is the greater value. Then the object governs the choice. I ask, in the above instance, had the mind any power or liberty to choose the object which appeared of the least value, and refuse that which appeared of the greatest? I am sure there is not a person in the world who would say that it had.

Again, admitting for the sake of the argument that the mind possesses this imaginary liberty; I then ask, how came it to possess such liberty? Answer, God gave it. Then the matter stands thus, God produced a mind, and gave it liberty to will, or choose, and it wills or chooses; I ask, what is the original cause of this willing and choosing? The reader will easily see, that if I grant my opponent's arguments, it will not be to his advantage.

Again, for the last time, if God gave to man a liberty whereby he can choose or refuse the same object, did he not give his creature a liberty which he did not possess himself? Did not the Infinitely Wise eternally know all that he himself would do? It must be granted. Then I ask again, does he possess any liberty in his nature, whereby it is in his power to abandon the general system contained in his divine omnisciency, and embrace one entirely different? I am sure there are but few in the world who would not say, as did the apostle, "He cannot deny himself." (2 Tim. ii. 13.) If the creature possess any ability which is not in his Creator, I would ask first, where he got it? And secondly, if the Almighty knew all the consequences which would arise from such an ability? If the answer be in the negative, it argues that his wisdom is finite and limited, and that he does not know but this unaccountable ability of willing and choosing may finally destroy his whole plan in creation, providence, and redemption! If it be granted that he did know all the consequences that would arise from this ability of willing and choosing, which is called liberty of will, it is denying its existence. For if those consequences are all known, it argues they were all certain, and none of them avoidable.

Having, as I hope to the reader's satisfaction, answered the objections in respect to the liberty of the will, I would again invite him back to our subject.

The immediate causes of sin are found in our natural constitutions, and the most distant of those immediate causes are the same as the most distant of the immediate causes of our virtues; but the most immediate causes of our virtues and our vices are extremely different. For instance, two men meet at an inn; both of them have families which are in want of bread; they have each fifty cents, which they have just taken for their day's work. One says to the other, Come, sit down, and we will take some drink for our comfort after a hard day's labor. The other reflects in his mind, and says to himself, To let my children suffer at home, to gratify my company in what is indifferent to me, would be abominable, having no particular appetite for spirits; he therefore refuses, bids his company good night, goes and purchases necessary provisions for his family, and goes home. He has done as a virtuous, honest husband ought to do. The other possesses a violent appetite for ardent spirits; the moment he comes where it is his want of it overpowers his love and duty to his family, the latter object being at a distance, and the former being nigh; he calls for drink until he spends his fifty cents, and then goes home to his expecting family intoxicated. In this, according to the scriptures, though he were a professed Christian, he is worse than an infidel.

In the mirror presented, the reader may see that those two men acted equally alike from their natural wants, appetites and passions. Had neither of them any wants, appetites, or passions, neither of them would have done any thing at all. They would not have labored for the money; and if they had the money, they would not have laid it out in any way possible. Therefore we see that want, appetite, and passion in one produced virtue, and in the other vice. But the still more immediate causes were not the same in both persons; and the consequences to them, in a moral sense, differ as much as did the most immediate circumstances which produced their conduct. One felt the approbation of a good conscience in having done what cool, dispassionate reason dictated; the other, as soon as his eyes are opened to see what he has done, is struck with condemnation for having violated the dictates of that law of prudence and equity of which he was susceptible.

A beggar influenced by hunger calls at the door of the affluent for food; he knows it is there; his appetite is good; the object magnifies to his senses; but by one who knows the love of property more than the want of food, he is sternly denied. The beggar prostrates himself and moves his suit in language of distress, reducing his petition to only a piece of bread; the covetous man is a little moved with some small feelings of compassion, but fearing that if he should bestow he should consequently be troubled again, bids the beggar depart, and leaves him. The beggar's object was food, and his passion hunger; he acted up to the influence of his object, and did all in his power to obtain it. The other's object was the saving of his property, and his passion was covetousness; he acted up to the influence of his object, to the gratification of his passion. Now had the circumstance been varied so much as this, that he did not think his giving at that time would ever induce him to call again, the probability is his object and his passion would both have been different; to feed a hungry man would have been his object, and charity his passion.

Man's main object in all he does is happiness; and were it not for that, he never could have any other particular object. What would induce men to form societies; to be at the expense of supporting government; to acquire knowledge; to learn the sciences, or to till the earth, if they believed they could be as happy without, as with? The fact is man would not be the being that he now is, as there would not be any stimulus to action; he must become inert, therefore cease to be. As men are never without this grand object, so they are never without their wants which render such an object desirable. But their minor objects vary, accordingly as their understanding vary, and their passions differ.

Then, says the objector, there is no such thing as disinterested benevolence. We answer, words are used to communicate ideas; there is that often in our experience which is meant by disinterested benevolence. An American is travelling in Europe; he meets, in the street, a young and beautiful fair lady, bathed in tears, her breast swollen with grief, and her countenance perfectly sad. His heart, fraught with the keenest sensibility, is moved compassionately to inquire the cause of her grief; he is informed that her father, in a late sickness, became indebted to his physician twenty guineas, for which he was that hour committed to jail, when he had but partially recovered his health. Our traveler no sooner hears the story than he advances the twenty guineas to discharge the debt, and gives her fifty more as a reward for her generous concern. As our traveler did not expect any pecuniary reward, either directly or indirectly, his charity is called disinterested benevolence. But strictly speaking, he was greatly interested; he was interested in the afflictions of father and child; their relief was his object; and charity his passion. Now did he not act for his own happiness? Yes, as much as ever a man did in life. What must have been his misery, possessing the same disposition, without the means to relieve? And what a sublime satisfaction he enjoyed by the bestowment of his favor! Sacred truth informs us, "It is more blessed to give, than to receive." (Acts xx. 35.)

We find some men honest and industrious; who think, and think justly, that happiness is not to be found in any other way. Others are indolent and knavish, and they expect to obtain happiness in so being. But they are deceived in their objects; and will finally learn that they must be what conscience has often told them they ought to be, honest and just, in order to be happy.

The objector will say: To admit that our happiness is the grand object of all we do destroys the purity of religion, and reduces the whole to nothing but selfishness. To which we reply, a man acting for his own happiness, if he seek it in the heavenly system of universal benevolence, knowing that his own happiness is connected with the happiness of his fellow men which induces him to do justly and to deal mercifully with all men, he is no more selfish than he ought to be. But a man acting for his own happiness, if he seek it in the narrow circle of partiality and covetousness, his selfishness is irreligious and wicked.

We know it is frequently contended that we ought to love God for what he is, and not for what we receive from him; that we ought to love holiness for holiness' sake, and not for any advantage such a principle is to us. This is what we have often been told, but what we never could see any reason for, or propriety in. I am asked if I love an orange; I answer, I never tasted of one; but am told I must love the orange for what it is! Now I ask, is it possible for me either to like or dislike the orange, in reality, until I taste it? Well, I taste of it, and like it. Do you like it? says my friend. Yes, I reply, its flavor is exquisitely agreeable. But that will not do, says my friend; you must not like it because its taste is agreeable, but you must like it because it is an orange. If there is any propriety in what my friend says, it is out of my sight.

A man is travelling on the sands of Arabia, he finds no water for a number of days; the sun scorches, and he is exceedingly dry; at last, he finds water and drinks to his satisfaction; never did water taste half so agreeably before. To say that this man loves the water because it is water, and not because of the advantage which he receives from it, betrays a large share of inconsistency. Would not this thirsty traveler have loved the burning sand as well as he did the water if it had tasted as agreeably, and quenched his thirst as well? The sweet Psalmist of Israel said, "O taste and see that the Lord is good." (Psalm xxxiv. 8.) And an apostle says, "We love him because he first loved us." (1 John iv. 19.) What attribute do we ascribe to God that we do not esteem on account of its advantage to us? Justice would have been no more likely to be attributed to the Almighty than injustice, if it had not first been discovered that justice was of greater advantage to mankind than injustice. And so of power, were it of no more advantage to human society than weakness; the latter would have been as likely to have been esteemed an attribute of God as the former. If wisdom were of no greater service to man than folly, it would not have been adored in the Almighty any more than folly. If the love were no more happifying to man than hatred, hatred would as soon have been esteemed an attribute of God as love.

Undoubtedly the Almighty loves without an influential object, as it would be erroneous to suppose that an infinite being could be operated upon. He loves because his nature is to love. An apostle says, "God is love." (1 John iv. 8.) The sun does not shine, because our earth influences it; it is the nature of the sun to shine. But all created beings love, because of influential objects; and they always love according to the influence which objects have on their minds and passions.

It seems then, says the objector, that our vices are not to be attributed to the devil, but to the influence which objects have on our minds. Surely the reader ought to expect that after we have denied the existence of a being, we should likewise deny his power. Perhaps, however, the reader may be surprised to find that we do not believe in the existence of a being so universally acknowledged among Christian people, and which perhaps has been of as much advantage to some, as the Goddess Dianna was to the craftsmen of Ephesus. But we are willing to give our reasons for not believing with the multitude in this particular.

A created individual being cannot be in more than one place at the same time. But how many millions of places must this evil angel be in at once in order to perform the business which Christians have allotted him? In order for us to believe in such a being, we must give him the omnipresency of the Almighty, which belongs to none, in my opinion, but our Maker. Again to admit the existence of such a being would be of no avail, as there is nothing for him to do. There is, says the objector; he tempts men to sin. But does he tempt men contrary to their passions and the influence of their motives? Answer, no. Then the temptation is of no possible consequence.

Supposing a man to be exceedingly hungry, and an agreeable meal is set before him, and he invited to refresh; at that moment, the devil comes, and tempts him to eat. What effect would the temptation have on the hungry man? Or supposing, in room of tempting him to eat, he should tempt him not to eat, would he be likely to succeed? But what means the scripture, which speaks of a devil? —one who was a liar from the beginning, etc. I answer, I have no objection to believing that there is such a devil as the scripture speaks of. He is called the old Serpent, and is the same I have described which beguiled the woman in the beginning; and it is the carnal mind which is enmity against God.

"I will put enmity between thee and the woman," said the Lord, "between her seed and thy seed." (Gen. iii. 15.) An apostle says, "The flesh lusteth against the spirit, and the spirit against the flesh, that ye cannot do the things ye would." (Gal. v. 17.) And, that this was the first beguiler, we may learn from the scripture, before quoted, which saith, "Lust, when it conceived, brought forth sin; and, sin when it was finished, brought forth death." (James i. 15.) An apostle also says, "When a man is tempted, he is drawn away with his own lusts, and enticed." (James i. 14.) Any person, who is wholly dictated by a fleshly mind, may justly be called a devil, as in the case of Judas and Peter. As our Lord said to the Jews, also, "Ye are of your father the devil; and the lusts of your father, ye will do." (John viii. 44.)

But, says the objector, do you think our Savior was tempted by the powers of the flesh when it was said he was tempted by the devil? I ask in my turn, for what is this particular circumstance introduced? If we cannot prove from our own experience that we are tempted by some other being than our own fleshly appetites, would it be any thing more than a speculative belief to admit another tempter?

But, says the objector, that does not answer the question. Then let us look at his temptations; when he hungered, he was tempted; by what? and to what? Answer, by hunger, to turn stones into bread. Here was a fleshly appetite. When he had a view of all the kingdoms of the earth and their worldly glory, he was tempted to avail himself of them. Here was natural ambition, such as gave rise to the victories of an Alexander. When on the pinnacle of the temple, he was tempted to cast himself down, as it was written concerning him, that God would give his angels charge over him, etc. (Matt. iv. 5-6.) Here was that passion which gives rise to presumption, and wishes to avoid duty. But, it is said, the devil taketh him about, thus and so; not literally, however, for there is no mountain in the world that commands a prospect of but a small part of the kingdoms of the world.

In a word, the scriptures inform us that he was tempted in all points as we are yet without sin. If, therefore, we know how we are tempted, we know also how he was tempted. It is a sentiment of mine that we ought not to argue that for truth in matters of this nature, of which we have no knowledge by experience.

Having illustrated the original cause, and the secondary causes of sin, I pass to take notice of its consequences.

3. Of Sin — Its consequences

In order to have our work plain before us, I observe, sin is the fruits of the flesh, which are opposed to that true light, which lighteth every man who cometh into the world. And St. Paul, as before quoted, says they are manifest; see Galatians v. 19-21:

> Now the works of the flesh are manifest which are these, adultery, fornication, uncleanness, lasciviousness, idolatry, witchcraft, hatred, variance, emulation, wrath, strife, seditions, heresies, envying, murders, drunkenness, revelings and such like.

These are the sins which our fleshly minds are daily producing, and their consequences are witnessed by a miserable world. By these sins, with their associates, mankind are rendered miserable indeed. Social and domestic happiness are frequently destroyed. Cold and cruel jealousy murders the soft and tender passions of love, as Cain slew his brother. A garden, enclosed by the walls of fidelity, decked with the flowers of innocence, watered with the living streams of love, teeming with fruits of richest repast, and adorned with the vine of future prospects, is laid waste in an hour. Jealousy, like a foe bent on plunder flung down the wall, dried up the stream, and, like a devouring worm, gnawed the vine, that it perished; the flowers droop, and the fruits wither away. Nothing remains but some faint vestiges of what is ruined, serving as evidence of the melancholy truth, that sin has found its way to this once happy place.

Idolatry is the sin of worshipping that which is not in reality the true God. The Old Serpent could never long hold the creature in captivity, if he did not allow him a god to worship, and religious duties to amuse him. Man is constituted in such relation to God that to worship is perfectly natural. Then, in order for the carnal mind to take the lead of the whole man, it must introduce a god to be worshipped, and religious duties whereby this god may be pleased, and make the creature believe that this god is the true god, and that those religious duties are of the genuine kind. But this god will surely possess all the vile passions of the old man, Adam, and those religious duties must consist in certain rites which bear no relation to heaven-born charity, or deeds of kindness. An Almighty, omnipresent, infinitely wise and good, may be talked of; but his wisdom, power, and goodness must be denied; and he must be a great many millions of miles off, fixed to a certain place, yet every where present; infinitely wise, and powerful, yet suffers an everlasting violation of his will; possessed of infinite wisdom, yet is disappointed in his plans; loves some of his creatures, and hates others; is pleased and displeased with the conduct of his creatures; is perfectly unchangeable, yet loves at one time, and at another hates the same object. Such an idol will answer for thousands.

Now what are the consequences? Answer, one nation supposes itself the only favorite of God; other people are haters of him, and hated by him. If our God hates those who hate him, we ought to do as our God does, and hate them too. One denomination of Christians has different ideas of the attributes of their God from another; they are violently opposed to each other; they are at swords' points; they call each other heretics, and doom each other to the endless wrath of their God! All such religion is of the flesh; the wisdom of it is not from above, but is earthly, sensual, and devilish, and those who possess it are tormented day and night with it.

Reader, turn over the pages of history, calculate the rivers of blood which have been shed on account of religious disputes, and ask yourself the question, Is this religion worthy of a Supreme Being? The devil will have religion, and will have it maintained as long as he can; but then he must tell the people that it is none of his, but that it came from the true and living God, or they will not believe it. It is an object with the Old Serpent to have a great many denominations, and to persuade them that they are individually right, and individually wrong, and to stir up their minds to maintain their respective tenets, and to wage war with each other, which he calls contending earnestly for the faith. Many who profess to be called by Him who loved sinners to preach his Gospel, and who pretend to follow the Savior in the path of meekness, if they happen to think a little differently in matters of faith they are filled with the greatest vehemency towards each other, which they call holy wrath, or indignation; and you might as well reason with hungry lions, or tigers, as with them, for they worship the beast and they partake largely of his nature. Did they worship the true God, in the spirit of the heavenly man, difference in particular sentiments would not hinder their fellowship and love of one another.

All the religion in our world, founded on the partial principles of man's inventions, pointing out particular modes of faith, and forms of worship, is from the carnal man. Discord and contention ensue; war and fightings are the consequences; hatred, wrath, strife, emulation, and rivalship, rage in the minds of those who possess this spurious religion. What I say is a truth of universal notoriety; and yet what is very strange is, people are not convinced of it. As if a monstrous wolf should ravage, in open day light, in the high and low parts of the shepherd's pasture, gorging his carnivorous appetite with the blood and fat of the flock; and the shepherd thinks it is all well, because somebody, on whose sleeve he pins his faith, has told him that that creature is a sheep and that it will do no harm! How miserable has religion made mankind!

But, says the reader, it was sin that you were to tell the consequences of, not religion. I tell you, kind reader, that the religion of which I speak is opposed to every decree of the spirit of life in Christ Jesus which has ever been revealed to mankind, and, therefore, is sin; and that which is attended with the most pernicious consequences. It is this kind of religion which takes away the "key of knowledge"; its votaries neither enter the kingdom of heaven themselves, nor suffer those to enter who would. All worship, which is dictated by modes and forms, as inventions of men, is opposed to the true worship. "The Father seeketh such to worship him ... who worship him in spirit and in truth." (John iv. 23, 24) Nothing suits the carnal mind better than religion; but it must be a child of her own, and must look just like herself. The carnal mind being the hot bed where all the roots of bitterness grow which trouble mankind, we ought to look there for the foundation of all that religion which bears the features of the serpent.

Pride is the most prominent characteristic of a fleshly mind; its religion dictates to look with contempt on those who are not of the same mode of faith, who do not subscribe to the same articles of belief, and are not called by the same denomination; and says, "Stand by thyself, come not nigh me, for I am holier than thou." (Isa. lxv. 5.) It dictates to give thanks for not being like others; it boasts of performances wrought with great pains and expense; it boasts of having "borne the burden and heat of the day" (Matt. xx. 12.) and dictates to expect more than others receive.

"But the carnal mind," says the reader, "makes no use of the scriptures, does it?" Always, be sure, where it is fashionable to believe them, and men are despised if they do not. Any thing will do, of which the creature is proud and is willing to persecute others for not adopting. But ought not men to be despised, and called all to naught, who do not believe the Bible to be the word of God? The Old Serpent will answer, yes, where it suits his turn best; but the spirit of Christ answers, no, in all cases. If the scriptures be not the word of God, men ought not to be despised for not believing them; and if they are they ought not to be despised, but pitied and enlightened. Remember, our acceptable High Priest was one who could "have compassion on the ignorant, and on them who were out of the way." (Heb. v. 2.)

Emulation, or rivalship, is one of the works of the flesh, and it is enmity against the meek and humble spirit of Christ; and its consequences are pernicious beyond description. In matters called religion we see much of its iniquity as well as in natural things. One denomination wishes to rival another; one preacher wishes to rival another; and how often is it the case, that professed Christians will act more underhandedly to obtain an advantage over a professor of a different denomination than a common jockey is willing to do in order to obtain a bargain. And I will say more, I have often seen in the same churches persons at such variance about matters of their religion that truth seemed not to be regarded in the least on either side; each would strive to crush his brother, until two parties were formed and a whole town sat in an uproar. This is the religion which pleases the carnal mind, but it is death.

One nation looks with an envious eye on the increasing wealth and population of another. She forms a subterfuge, as a pretext for declaring war against her neighbor, by which the two nations are drawn into a contention; a long war ensues, bringing horrors to describe which would swell a volume to an enormous size. Look on France and England this moment, and for many years back. Who could calculate one half the miseries produced from the spirit of rivalship between these potent rivals? How many brave youth have fallen a sacrifice to ambition; how often has the ground drunk copious draughts of human blood; the bosom of the deep been reddened with the gore of the slain; and Sharks and Sea Dogs fed on the sons of mourning fathers and weeping mothers; while the leaders of this calamity make high professions of the religion of the meek and lowly Jesus, and are frequently sending out their proclamations for fasts, and for prayers to Almighty God, to assist them in human butchery! "From whence come wars and fightings among you? come they not even from your lusts, which war against the soul?" (James iv. 1.)

It is recorded in the scriptures that the love of money is the root of all evil. But men would have no love for money were it not for the earthly advantages obtained by it. Then the passion is covetousness, and the consequence is mischievous to mankind. One, for the sake of money, will steal, another will lie, another counterfeit the currency, and another will murder. Were it not for the sake of property, would men do these things? Answer, no. Then, in relation to what I have before argued, I ask, would men be industrious were it not for the sake of property? Answer, no; then the case is plain that they both act from the same main passion, which is want, and to the same main object, which is happiness. But their minor objects and their minor passions vary. What need would there be of government, were it not for sin? If all were willing to do as they would be done by, what an enormous expense would be saved; as it would render governmental laws useless. But by reason of men's passions, and mistaken objects influencing them, our lives are exposed to be taken by our neighbors, our property pillaged, our hard earnings wrung by violence away, and our midnight slumbers interrupted by banditti, and, in short, all that is dear to us to be taken from our enjoyment.

"He who loveth not his brother, is a murderer." (1 John iv. 20.) Are not all men murderers? —do they not sometimes experience the lack of brotherly love? This murderous passion is sin, it is opposed to the language of the heavenly man in the mind; but what are its consequences? Everyone endeavors to supplant his brother; no one is safe in his feelings while he is in the hands of his brother. When this passion reigns, all the tender charities of humanity are suppressed; all "the bowels of compassion are frozen" (1 John iii. 17); a deaf ear is turned to the cries and calls of the needy in distress; the poor are despised by the rich, the rich are envied by the poor; parents are dishonored by their children; children are abused, and provoked to anger by their parents. The vile affections of sin will burn to the destruction of the sweetest harmonies of nature; the whitest robes of innocence are stained with its indelible crimson; the soul is drowned in the black waters of iniquity, and the whole mind, with every faculty, is plunged into the hell of moral death.

Yet listen to the worst of torments in consequence of sin. "A wounded conscience, who can bear?" (Prov. xviii. 14.) A fire that burns all the day long, a sword that continually pierceth the soul, a sting that cannot exhaust its poison, a fever that never turns till the patient dies. "A dart struck through his liver." (Prov. vii. 23.) What ails the sinner? —why his hand on his breast? There gnaws the worm that never dies, there burns the fire that is never quenched. A consciousness of guilt destroys all the expected comforts and pleasures of sin. How strange it is that after a thousand disappointments in succession, men are not discouraged. O sin! how you paint your face; how you flatter us, poor mortals, on to death; you never appear to the sinner in your true character; you make us fair promises, but you never fulfilled one; your tongue is smoother than oil, but the poison of asps is under your lips; you have impregnated all our passions with the venom of your poison; you have spread gloomy darkness over the whole region of the soul; you have endeavored, with your stupefactive poison, to blunt the sword in the hands of the cherubims, which, for your sake, keeps us from the tree of life.

A mistaken idea has been entertained of sin, even by professors. I have often heard sincere ministers preach, in their reproofs to their hearers, that it was the greatest folly in the world for people to forego salvation in a future state for the comforts and pleasures of sin in this. Such exhortations really defeat their intentions. The wish of the honest preacher is that the wicked should repent of their sins, and do better; but at the same time, he indicates that sin at present is more productive of happiness than righteousness; but that the bad will come in another world, that although doing well is a hard way, yet its advantages will be great in another state. Just as much as any person thinks sin to be more happifying than righteousness, he is sinful; his heart esteems it though in some possible cases, for fear of the loss of salvation in the world to come, he may abstain from some outward enormities; yet his heart is full of the desire of doing them. A thief passes a merchant's shop, wishes to steal some of his goods, but durst not, for fear of apprehension and punishment. Is this man less a thief at heart, for not actually taking the goods?

I have been told by persons of high professions in Christianity, that if they were certain of salvation in the world to come they would commit every sin to which their unbridled passions might lead them; even from the lips of some who profess to preach the righteousness of Christ, have I heard such-like expressions! I do not mention these things to cast reflections on any person or denomination in the world; for I have a favorable hope that there are some in all denominations who are not so deceived; but I mention them in order to show how deceiving sin is to the mind.

It is as much the nature of sin to torment the mind, as it is the nature of fire to burn our flesh. Sin deprives us of every rational enjoyment so far as it captivates the mind; it was never able to furnish one drop of cordial for the soul; her tender mercies are cruelty, and her breasts of consolation are gall and wormwood. Sin is a false mirror by which the sinner is deceived in every thing on which his mind contemplates. If he think of his Maker, who is his best friend, it strikes him with awe, fills his mind with fearful apprehensions, and he wishes there was no such being. If he think of any duty which he owes his Maker, he says in a moment, God is a hard master; why should he require of me what is so contrary to my happiness? Religion is only calculated to make men miserable; righteousness blunts my passions, and deprives me of pleasures for which I long. But it represents stolen waters to be sweet, and bread eaten in secret to be pleasant. In a word, sin is of a torment-giving nature to every faculty of the soul, and is the moral death of the mind.

Well, says the reader, can sin have all those evil effects, and not be infinite? Undoubtedly; as all those evil effects are experienced in this finite state. Thousands who, I hope, are gone to greater degrees of rest than the most upright enjoy here, were once tormented with sin, were once under the dominion of the carnal mind. The effects of sin, as sin, are not endless, but limited to the state in which it is committed. This perhaps will be contrary to the opinion of many who read this treatise, as they are wont to suppose that there are three cardinal consequences produced by sin, viz.: death temporal, death spiritual, and death eternal.

As to the first of these consequences, I say: Men die natural deaths because they are naturally mortal; but they are not mortal because of sin, for man was mortal before he sinned; if he were not, he never could have sinned. My opponent will say that the death of the body is the consequence of sin when one man murders another; to which I reply, one man could not murder another if men were not mortal. Sin cannot be said to be the cause of natural death, any more than of natural life. I will acknowledge that sin is often the means whereby natural life is ended, and my opposer must acknowledge that it is often the means of persons being introduced into natural life. Perhaps a hundred are introduced into existence by illicit connections, where one is taken out by *malice prepense*. But the meaning of the objector is that man became mortal by sin; to which I reply, if immortality be corruptible by sin, the Christian hope of immortality is a vain one. The death which Adam died in consequence of sin happened on the day of transgression, if we may believe the scripture account about it; but Adam did not die a natural death on that day, nor for some hundreds of years afterwards.

The way in which many have tried to reconcile the scriptures with their traditions, in this matter, appears strange to us; they quote 2 Peter iii. 8:

> But, beloved, be not ignorant of this one thing, that one day with the Lord, is as a thousand years, and a thousand years as one day;

and as Adam died short of a thousand years, he died in the day of transgression. But, in order for the text to read to their meaning, it ought to read thus, "One day with the Lord is a thousand years, and a thousand years is one day" (2 Peter iii. 8); as they understand the text, the conjunction *as* has no possible meaning. In respect to spiritual death, I believe it was all that was meant by the word, "in the day thou eatest thereof thou shalt surely die." (Gen. ii. 17.) But if eternal death were also intended, there was no recovery for man.

Why divines have carried this matter so erroneously beyond all scripture testimony, we cannot imagine. But, it is said, spiritual or moral death would be eternal were it not for the dispensation of the Gospel, by which death is swallowed up of life. So we might say of any thing else, even of a momentary nature, it would be eternal if it were never to end. The days of a man's life would be eternal, if they were never to end. The spring would be eternal, if it were not succeeded with the summer. A rose would be an eternal flower, if it never withered. And youth would be eternal, if it were not for old age and death. But what do all such arguments avail? The grand, sublime, and glorious system of God carries everything away that has its birth from mortality and time.

I have already hinted that sin might have consequences which were not evil, but not as sin. By the infinite wisdom and goodness of the Almighty, sin may be of advantage even to the sinner himself; but I say again, not as sin. If the infinitely Wise and Good intended any one thing for good which we rightly call sin, that event in respect to the divine intention is not sin. I have introduced a circumstance in the fore part of this work in which what we are now endeavoring to illustrate may clearly be seen. It is evident that that which Joseph's brethren meant unto evil, God meant unto good. Now the immediate consequences of their sin, to them, was guilt of the first magnitude. Who could calculate the one half of what they endured in consequence of the wrong which they had done? But the consequences which God intended in the issue of the event were altogether beneficial; and those who committed the sin, by the mercy of God, were made the partakers of the benefits contained in the purpose of him who meant it for good.

Again, it is evident from the scriptures that Herod, Pontius Pilate, the Gentiles, and the people of Israel were gathered together against Jesus to do what the council and the hand of the Almighty had determined to be done; see Acts iv. 27-28. Had Herod, Pontius Pilate, the Gentiles, and the people of Israel any better meaning in crucifying Christ than Joseph's brethren had in selling Joseph to the Ishmaelites? All who read the question will answer, no. But the sacred text says they were gathered together to do whatsoever God's hand and council had determined to be done. Now I ask, was not the determination of the murderers of Christ the same with the determination of Divine Wisdom? Says the reader, I cannot say it was not, and yet I dare not say it was. I will then answer, the Almighty intended all they did, should be done; but he intended it for a very different purpose from what they did, who did it. They intended the destruction and overthrow of the doctrine which Christ preached, and they hoped the things which he had spoken concerning them would fail of taking place. But the means which they used to oppose the cause of Christ were those with which God intended to promote it. They missed of their intentions, and the Lord carried the whole of his into effect. What Christian is there in the world who will say the consequences of the death of Christ are not good? —or that those who were his murderers, for whom he prayed on the cross, will not receive an advantage from his death, which they meant for evil? Or who can limit the good contained in the designs of the Almighty?

But will this rule do, says the reader, to apply to all sin? I answer without hesitancy that we fully believe it. Food for the body would never please the appetite unless we first experienced hunger; the cooling spring would not be sought for if men were never thirsty; health could never be prized could we not contrast it with sickness; ease is appreciated by the remembrance of pain; and a physician would never be wanted if it were not for our infirmities; a Savior would never have been praised by his redeemed had they never been in bondage; the song, "Thou hast redeemed us to God, out of every kingdom and nation" (Rev. v. 9), could never be sung had redemption not been needed; a fountain would never have been opened for Judah and Jerusalem to wash in, from sin and uncleanness, had it not been for sin and uncleanness.

Then, says our opponent, we may do evil that good may come. This objection has often been stated to me in conversation on this subject. My reply is short: There is a self-contradiction in the objection; to do anything whatever for good, is not a moral transgression. Had Joseph's brethren been taught of God that it was necessary for them to sell Joseph to the Ishmaelites, that he might go down to Egypt and there prepare for the famine, and they had done it for the good which God intended, it would have been no more sin in them than there was in the design of God. Then it is plain, that to do evil that good may come is impossible.

Again, had Herod, Pontius Pilate, the Gentiles, and the people of Israel intended the good which God intended in the crucifixion of Christ, sin would have been out of the question. St. Paul asks the question to his opposers, after he had argued that where sin abounded grace did much more abound: "Shall we continue in sin, that grace may abound?" (Rom. vi. 1.) And answers it thus, God forbid. How shall we, who are dead to sin, live any longer therein? If we are truly enlightened into the nature of the all-abounding grace of the Gospel, it causes us to die to sin; and if we are dead to sin, we shall not live in it. God has forbidden it, in the nature of things, and rendered it impossible.

As I have limited sin in its nature, the reader will not expect to find unlimited consequences attached to it in this work. Were it so, that the fullness of the divine law was perfectly comprehended in the mind of the creature and he should go contrary thereto, his sin would then be as infinite as the law transgressed; but I argue that the law transgressed is a law formed in the mind of an imperfect being by the imperfect knowledge which he obtains of the divine law, which is no other than God himself. This knowledge being imperfect, it forms a law like itself, imperfect and mutable; and an imperfect, mutable law does not afford data from which to argue endless consequences. The sacred oracle declares, "the soul that sins shall die" (Eze. xviii. 20); if it had added, "and shall never live again," it would have carried the consequences of sin infinitely farther than the Holy Ghost intended. Sin is death to the soul as long as it sins, be that time longer or shorter. In order to argue an endless consequence, we must first state an infinite cause; and as I have argued sin on a finite scale, and in a limited circle, we must rationally limit its consequences.

I will now state two particulars which the reader will find argued in the course of this work, state my opponent's objections against them, answer those objections, and introduce my second general inquiry, by stating a third objection.

First: Man is dependant in all his volitions, and moves by necessity.

Second: The Almighty has a good intention, in every volition of man.

Objection first: If man move by necessity, why do the scriptures abound with exhortations and admonitions to dissuade from sin, and so many inducements to persuade to holiness and virtue? And why are there requirements in the law, to which man is under the necessity of going contrary?

Objection second: If God has a good intention in every action or volition of man, why is it said in the scriptures that he is grieved and provoked with us? etc.

The proposition against which the first objection stands answers the objection in all its parts. It was in the system of divine wisdom that man should experience a consciousness of sin and guilt, without which the subject of my inquiry could never have existed. If sin and guilt had never been introduced into our system, the plan of grace by atonement could never have been exhibited. Sin and guilt could never have existed, providing there had been no prohibition communicated to the intelligent mind; and, on the other hand, if the mind possessed as much liberty to go contrary to inducements as it does inclination to follow them, inducements would have no possible effect; exhortations, admonitions, and warnings would be of no possible service.

If God purposed that man should come to the knowledge of his own infirmities in the way that he does, he must have intended all the means whereby the purpose might be accomplished. And if he designed that any degree of moral holiness should be found on earth, such inducements must influence the minds of men which would necessarily produce it. That God does in a strict sense of speaking require more of any of his creatures than they are able to perform is inconsistent with the dictates of good, of reason, and destitute of scripture authority; and has no better foundation for its support than an idea that darkness originates in the sun, or light in an opaque body.

But does not God require perfect holiness of man? Does he not command strict obedience, to every jot and tittle of his law? I have before argued that the spirit of God's law, in its infinite fullness, was above the capacity of man in a finite state in which he was made subject to vanity; and that it was a limited knowledge of the law only that was introduced to the creature's understanding, and that for the purpose that the offence might abound. Then, says my opponent, if you are correct in this statement, does it not prove that the requirement is more than the abilities of the creature can perform? And how can the difficulty be removed?

The proper answer to this question is derived from a due recurrence to the original constitution of man. If I believe that man as a moral being was constituted to occupy this mortal state only, and that his whole existence is limited to this state, then must I conclude that in this mortal state when I find health and sickness, pleasure and pain, virtue and vice, happiness and misery, the law of moral rectitude, all being obeyed so far as to correspond with the law of physical organization which is productive of the natural health of the body, it answers the full extent of its purposes and is as fully obeyed as the Creator designed it ever should be. It is evident that the designs of the Creator in the laws of corporeal or animal nature embrace not only all the health and pleasure which corporeal beings enjoy; but also all the sickness and pain they endure. So likewise in this constitution of man as a moral being, the law of moral rectitude was designed to administer not only those moral enjoyments which are far the sweetest felicities with which we are blessed, but also those pungent compunctions of conscience which are our bitterest sufferings. If therefore I extend my views no farther than man's earthly state, I view it perfectly philosophical to conclude that it was no more the design of the Creator that man should here enjoy perfect righteousness free from the alloys of guilt, than it was that he should here enjoy uninterrupted health and ease of body.

But in agreement with my view, before expressed, concerning man's original constitution as a moral being, in which he was made subject to vanity by reason of him who subjected him in hope, I embrace the doctrine of future, immortal life; in which state man will be as free from sin and condemnation, as that immortal state will be free from sickness, corruption, and death.

We, according to their views, look for present obedience to the divine law in that glorious constitution manifested in Christ, who hath abolished death, and brought life and immortality to light through the Gospel, and who is said, to be, the Lord our righteousness.

I come to take notice of the second objection. There are many passages of scripture which represent the Almighty as possessing irritable passions like his creatures. We are told that it repented him that he had made man on the earth, and that it grieved him at the heart. These expressions are as strong in their indication of changeability as any that might be chosen. An apostle exhorts not to grieve the Holy Spirit; and it is not infrequent that God is provoked to anger and jealousy, according to scripture. My opponent will not argue that we ought to understand those scriptures as strictly and literally true; no man, in his senses, can believe them so, and yet believe the Almighty unchangeable.

Supposing my opponents should give their own opinion of this question; I have no doubt but they would remove the objection, to all intents. I understand those scriptures, as many others do, to be spoken according to the dark understanding of man who is ignorant of the real character of God; and according to the representations made by the law to the unreconciled mind. To admit, in a strict sense of speaking, that God was ever grieved to the heart for what he did himself, or for what his creatures do, is more than I can do, and believe in the perfections of his.

St. James says, With God there is no variableness nor shadow of turning. (James 1.17.) This expression is as strong an indication of the unchangeability of the Almighty as any that might be chosen. St. Paul informs us that God works all things after the council of his own will. Our being led by a carnal and fleshly mind, is undoubtedly what the apostle meant, by grieving the Holy Spirit; as the motions or volitions of the carnal man are opposed to those of the heavenly; but that the eternal Spirit of God ever felt grief is more than we can rationally admit, as that would reduce the Almighty to a state of suffering.

It is very evident, that the scriptures represent the Almighty in extremely different characters; and we confess we cannot reconcile them in any other way than by the two covenants, or what is the same, flesh and spirit. Our ideas of God, while under the legal dispensation, walking in fleshly minds, are consonant to that character which the scripture represents our Creator in, as wrathful, filled with indignation towards us for our sins, and every day angry. Those ideas which the mind entertains of the father of all mercies when enlightened by the spirit of the new man, and while walking in the spirit of life in Christ Jesus, which maketh free from the law of sin, are altogether consonant to that endearing character given in scripture, of our Father who is in heaven, who causeth his sun to shine on the evil and on the good; and sendeth rain upon the just, and upon the unjust; who loved us while we were yet enemies, and sent his Son to die in attestation of his love to his creatures; who is good unto all, and whose tender mercies are over all his works; who is of one mind, and changeth not.

Says my opponent, if the Almighty govern all the affairs of mankind, according to his own appointment; if he were never disappointed; suffers no violation of will; but does in all things, and by all things, maintain and support his own eternal system of divine goodness, what room do we find for the necessity of atonement, whereby peace is made by the blood of the cross?

By this question, I come to my second general subject, viz., atonement for sin.

PART TWO: ATONEMENT FOR SIN

In our inquiries on this momentous subject, we shall:

First: Examine three doctrinal tenets on atonement; from which we shall beg leave to dissent, and give our reasons therefor.

Secondly: Show the necessity of atonement, and where satisfaction must be made.

Thirdly: Inquire into the personage and character of the Mediator, who makes the atonement, and his ability to perform the work.

Fourthly: Inquire of atonement in its nature.

4. Erroneous Theories of Atonement

Christian divines, in general, have agreed in supposing sin to be an infinite evil, being a violation of an infinite law, and therefore that the law required an infinite sacrifice; short of which no atonement could be made that the transgression of Adam brought the whole human race into the same situation of sin and misery, and subjected them all to the infinite penalty of an infinite law, which they had violated in their parent before they individually existed.

After the above agreement many different roads are taken; and divines of the greatest abilities, and of the first rank among the literati, have drained the last faculty of invention in plodding through the dark regions of metaphysics to bring up a Samuel to explain the solecism of satisfying an infinite dissatisfaction.

The plan of redemption, as held by many, may be reduced to the following compendium. God, from all eternity, foreseeing that man would sin, provided a Mediator for a certain part of his posterity, who should suffer the penalty of the law for them, and that those elect ones, chosen by God from the rest of mankind, will alone be benefited by the atonement; that in order that the sacrifice might be adequate to the crime for which the sinner was condemned to everlasting or endless suffering, God himself assumed a body of flesh and blood, such as the delinquent was constituted in, and suffered the penalty of the law by death, and arose from the dead. By this process, the demand of the law was completely answered, and the debt due to Divine Justice by the elect was fully and amply paid. But that this atonement does not affect those who were not elected as objects of mercy, but that they are left to suffer endlessly for what Adam did before they were born. It is true that they are a little cautious about saying that God himself absolutely died! But they say that Christ, who was crucified, was really God himself, which must, in effect, amount to the same thing. And in fact if the Infinite did not suffer death, the whole plan fails, for it is by an infinite sacrifice that they pretend to satisfy an infinite dissatisfaction.

Why the above ideas should ever have been imbibed by men of understanding and study, I can but scarcely satisfy myself; their absurdities are so glaring that it seems next to impossible that men of sobriety and sound judgment should ever imbibe them or avoid seeing them.

I have already sufficiently refuted the idea of an infinite sin, which opens to a plain path in which the mind may run, and run clear of all those perplexities which have served to confuse rather than enlighten mankind.

If sin is not infinite, the dissatisfaction occasioned by sin is not infinite, therefore an infinite sacrifice is not required. But, for the sake of illustration, we will for a moment admit that the doctrine of atonement stands on the ground over which we have just gone. I will state it as it is often stated by those who believe it, which is by the likeness of debt and credit. The sinner owed a debt to Divine Justice which he was unable to discharge; the Divine Being cannot, consistently with his honor, dispense with the pay, but says I must have my due; but as the debtor has not ability to pay the smallest fraction, Divine Wisdom lays a deep concerted mysterious plan for the debt to be discharged. And how was it? Why, for God to pay it himself!

My neighbor owes me a hundred pounds; time of payment comes, and I make a demand for my dues. Says my neighbor, my misfortunes have been such that I am not the possessor of the smallest fraction of property in the world; and as much as I owe you I am worse than nothing. I declare to him, positively, that I will not lose so much as a fraction of the interest, and leave him. A friend calls and asks me how I succeeded in obtaining my dues of my neighbor; I reply, my neighbor is not, nor will he ever be able to pay me any part of my demand. My friend says he is sorry that I should lose my debt. I answer, I shall not lose it. I have very fortunately, in my meditations on the subject, thought of a method by which I can avail myself of the whole to my full satisfaction; and I think it is a method which no person in the world, but myself, could have ever discovered. My friend is curious and impatient to know the mighty secret never before found out. The reader may guess his confusion on my telling him that as I have the sum already by me, I am now going to pay up the obligation before the interest is any larger! This has been called the Gospel plan, which contains the depths of infinite wisdom.

I should be pleased to see, what I have never seen, professors following such an example in obtaining what the poor widow, the fatherless, and the needy, owe them. But, says the advocate for the plan, a distinction should be made between the persons in the Godhead. It was the second person in the Godhead who paid this infinite debt to the first; therefore it is not altogether like a person paying his own demand. I say, in answer, if the first and second persons in the Godhead are not so essentially one as to make the debts due to one belong equally to the other, and payment also, they are not so essentially one as to be represented by two distinct persons related only by Adam, who are in company in merchandise.

But for the sake of carrying the argument still further, I will admit this variety of persons in an infinite, indivisible being! And also the plan of atonement on the principle of the second person's paying the demand to the first. And here it will be necessary to introduce the third person in the Godhead, as it is contended that the third person makes known to the debtor what the creditor determines concerning him. Then the plan of the doctrine may be represented by the following similitude:

A owes B the sum of one thousand pounds; the time of payment comes, demand is made. A is not worth a farthing, neither is it in his power to raise a fraction of the money. B immediately commences a process against A, of which C, a friend of A's, being informed, goes to B, asks him how large a demand he holds against A. B informs him, a thousand pounds and interest. And A is worth nothing? asks C. Nothing, answers B. Would you make a deduction of twenty-five per cent. if you could have the money down? asks C. Not the least deduction, answers B. Well, says C, if will have no mercy on the poor and distressed, I will have the pleasure of relieving the debtor alone; counts out the money in full, and receives the obligation of bestow on his friend A.

B sends a servant to immediately inform A that he has concluded to forgive him the debt. A is transported at the news, flies to tell his wife and children the tidings of mercy, and all join in praising such heavenly benevolence. C comes in, the same moment, with the obligation in his hand, modestly gives it to A, desiring him to accept it as a token of undissembled friendship. A is confounded, asks C how he came by the obligation. C informs him that he paid every farthing of the money for it, the creditor would not make the least deduction.

I leave the reader to judge whether the creditor showed any mercy to the debtor, and whether B's pretensions of favoring A do not wear the appearance of hypocrisy. It is contended by those who hold to this debt and the payment of it, that the salvation of the sinner is by being forgiven; yet they contend that the debt was paid. But how I can forgive a man a debt, and oblige him to pay it, is more that I can see.

Again, admitting the system true, I wish to inquire into the propriety of an innocent person's suffering for one who is guilty. It is Scripture, reason, and good law never to condemn the innocent in order to exculpate the delinquent. Supposing a foreign court sends a person who is old in conspiracies and blood to America, to lay a deep concerted plan to murder the President of the Union and a number of the first officers in the Federal government, for purposes mischievous to our political existence; and he should so far succeed as to engage a number in this wicked design, and finally makes the attempt: his plans are discovered by government and detected, but not until numbers have fallen a sacrifice to his mischievous endeavors. The leader of these seditious murderers is taken and condemned to be executed; and the voice of every friend of justice and equity is against the criminal.

But what would be the consternation of the good people of the United States on being informed that the good president of the Union, the man whom the people delighted to honor, was executed in the room of this seditious person, and the wicked murderer set at liberty? Is it possible to conceive that there is a single person in the world who would call this a just execution? If it be said that the president freely offered himself in the room of the criminal, it alters not the case in the eye of justice. If an innocent man can justly be put to death because he consents to it willingly, a guilty one may be acquitted because he prefers it.

But it is further argued that the authority had power to raise the president from the dead, which done, renders the work just and glorious. I say, in answer, that if the authority had this power, it might as well have executed the real criminal and raised him from the dead, as to perform this work on one who was not guilty. What is the most shocking of anything in this system of atonement is the partiality represented in the Almighty; for admitting the plan rational, as it respects those circumstances in which I have shown its absurdity, what can we find in Scripture or reason that justifies such infinite partiality in our Creator? or what can, in the least, serve as evidence to prove him possessed of it? have we not reason to believe our Creator possessed of as much goodness as he has communicated to us? Can we rationally believe that he is wanting in those principles of goodness which he has placed in our understanding? When he saw the whole progeny of Adam in the same situation of sin, no one more guilty than another, why should he propose a plan of mercy for some few of them and disregard the rest?

The sacred oracle declares God to be no respecter of persons; if this be true he is not a partial being. Jesus taught the character of God to his disciples by turning their attention to nature, observing the equal distribution of rain and sunshine on the evil and the good, on the just and on the unjust. Supposing Joseph had dealt out bread plentifully to two of his brethren in Egypt, and had starved the rest to death, would it have looked like impartiality? It is argued that none of them deserved a crumb from Joseph, whom they had sold; and if he pleased to give to one and not to the other, he had a right so to do. Then, I say, he had a right to be partial.

I am travelling through a large and extensive wood, and many miles from any inhabitant; I find ten persons who are lost; they have been out of provisions from several days; and having fatigued themselves in wandering from hill to hill, from stream to stream, striving to the utmost of their minds, they bid wives and children a long farewell, they are waiting for hunger to do its last work! The moment I discover myself to them, with large supplies of wholesome and rich provisions, every eye glistens with unexpected joy; the current of life starts afresh in their veins, and they all advance to meet me on their enfeebled hands and knees, with eagerness to receive the staff of life! I hasten to improve the opportunity of showing my sovereign and goodness; I feed five of them to the full, the other five I neglect. They beg for the smallest crust, which I do not want, but to no effect. Those whom I feed solicit me, every mouthful they eat, to bestow some on their fellow-sufferers, but I refuse. I tell them, however, not to construe my conduct into partiality, but to learn my power and sovereignty by it. The five whom I have fed I assist out of the wood, and leave the rest to their wants. My conduct in the above affair appears so much blacker than my paper is white, I choose rather to leave the reader to make his comments than to write my own.

I inquire still further, did the Almighty know, before he made man, that man would become a sinner? Did God know that man would deserve an endless punishment? If the answer be in the negative, it supposed God to be wanting in knowledge, and that he created beings at an infinite risk, as he did not know what would be the consequences. If the question be answered in the positive, it proves that an infinite cruelty existed in God; for unless that was the case he would never have created beings who he knew would be infinitely the losers by their existence.

Those who believe in the system which I am examining, believe in the existence of the devil, whose existence I have refuted in this work. I am willing, however, for the sake of the argument, to admit the existence of their God and devil likewise. But I wish to inquire which of them is, in reality, the worst being. God, when he created mankind, perfectly knew that some of them would suffer endless torment for their sins; he must, therefore, have intended them for that purpose; and his purpose could not be contrary to his knowledge. The matter then stands thus: God created millions of beings for endless misery, which they could not escape; the devil is desirous of having them miserable, and does all in his power to effect it. Now, reader, judge between these two beings. Had this devil been consulted by the Almighty when he laid the plan of man's final destiny, I cannot conceive him capable of inventing one more eligible to his infernal disposition than this which I am now disputing.

As reason will not consent to the plan of God as described in the foregoing scheme, I will show that Scriptures equally oppose it. It is granted that Jesus Christ died for mankind, as the Scriptures declare; but not in the way in which thousands have believed. But supposing he died instead of the sinner, in the way which I dispute, I still wish to prove that he died for the whole of Adam's posterity as much as he did not any. If Isaiah did not believe that that would be the case, I cannot reconcile his words to his opinion, which I find in chap. liii. 5-6:

> But he was wounded for our transgressions, he was bruised for our iniquities; the chastisement of our peace was upon him; and with his stripes we are healed. All we, like sheep, have gone astray: We have turned every one to his own way; and the Lord hath laid on him the iniquity of us *all*.

St. Paul must have been of this opinion when he wrote to Timothy, or his words are not expressive of his belief; see 1 Tim. ii. 5-6:

> For there is one God, and one Mediator between God and men, the man Christ Jesus; who gave himself a ransom for all to be testified in due time.

1st General Epistle of John ii. 1-2:

> My little children, these things write I unto you, that ye sin not, and if any man sin, we have an advocate with the Father, Jesus Christ the righteous; and he is the propitiation for our sins, and not for ours only, but also the sins of the whole world.

Heb. ii. 9:

> But we see Jesus, who was made a little lower than the angels, for the suffering of death, now crowned with glory and honor; that he, by the grace of God, should taste death for every man.

The above Scriptures, with their connections and corresponding passages, as fully prove that Christ dies for all men, as any one thing can be proved from the Bible. Now, as there is not in all the Scripture a single hint to the reverse of these passages which I have introduced, it appears strange and unaccountable to me that any person who professes to believe the testimony of the Bible should ever have entertained the idea that what these passages say is false, and that which is not said, in contradiction to what is, is true!

Look, ye readers, and submit to astonishment at what has been believed in as divine truth. An almighty, infinitely wise and good being creates an innumerable multitude of rational intelligences; they rebel against him, and raise an infinite dissatisfaction in his mind toward them; this infinite dissatisfaction gets removed toward part of the offenders by the sacrifice of innocence! With the rest, God is still displeased; yet he is almighty and infinitely wise and employs his power and wisdom to make the works of his own hand as miserable as their natures will bear, for being just such creatures as he knew they would be, before he made them.

But it is argued that God's knowing what sort of creatures men would be did not influence them in the smallest degree to be what they are. Let this argument be granted. But did not God know what would influence men to be what they are? Answer, yes. Was it in his power to remove this influential cause? If it were, why did he not do it, if it were like to displease him? If it were not in his power to prevent the mischief, we wish to know whether it were in the creature's power to prevent it? If it were not in the power of either of them to prevent the operation of things in the way in which they have, and do, take place, why is God's anger so warm against his poor impotent offspring?

It seems an unhappy circumstance for both Creator and creature. The Creator is not satisfied with his creatures; his creatures find themselves introduced into an existence infinitely worse than none. I am born into this world of sorrow and trouble; the first vibration of sense is want; I endeavor to supply my wants, and to maintain my existence, which my Maker has bestowed upon me; but as soon as I come to years of understanding, I am told of an infinite debt which stands against me, which I owed thousands of years before I was born; and that my Maker is so angry with me, and has been ever since the debt was due, that he has prepared a furnace of endless flames to torment me in, according to the due requirements of justice!

My father gives me his farm, and puts me in possession of it; I am pleased, and prize it very highly. In consequence of my possession, I paint to myself many pleasing prospects; but, to my mortification, a person comes and presents me with a mortgage of my farm for five times its value, the mortgage running so as to hold the possessor to clear it; I will leave the reader to say whether my father was kind or unkind. Yet the circumstance into which the Almighty has introduced millions of his creatures is infinitely worse according to the doctrine which we are examining.

It is argued, with much assurance, that God has a just right to do with his creatures as he pleases, because he has it in his power so to do; and that he never does anything because it is right; but what he does is right, because he does it. If the above statement is just, moral holiness consists in the power of action, and not in the disposition that designs the action. If so, my argument in favor of sin's existing only in the design of the actor, and not in the action, is groundless; and we are driven to say that unholiness, or sin, is the want of power to perform an action; and holiness consists in having the power to do it. One man designs to murder another for his money, he makes the attempt, and fails; his sin consisted in not having power to execute his design; but in the design there is no evil. On the other hand, he makes the attempt, and succeeds; here is no evil at all, because he had power to do it. On this principle, everything that can be done, is moral holiness; and every thing that cannot be done, is sin, or moral evil.

Here we are presented with a picture the most to be dreaded of anything which the imagination of man is capable of inventing. Power moving on in front, exhibiting tyrannic majesty in every action; and meager justice in the rear, obsequiously pronouncing all is right! If these things be so, our senses are nothing but mediums of deception; and all our experience has served us no other purpose than to make us more ignorant. Who is there in the world, possessing common sense, that does not dread and revolt from power in every instance where they see it connected with an evil disposition? Are we right in wishing our enemies weak? We are, and that because their strength being directed by their wicked designs gives us fear.

But, for the sake of the argument still further, let it be granted that, God being supreme, had a right to do because he had the power. And he creates millions of beings, whom he intends for endless torments, and puts his whole design into execution; and this is called supreme goodness. Now we wish to know how a supreme evil could be described? All will grant that evil is in opposition to good; then an opposite description would be just. To create, with an intention to make eternally happy, and to put that design into execution, would be supreme evil! But, according to the doctrine which I am examining, God contains these two characters in himself, having created some for one purpose, and some for the other. It will be of no advantage to the reader to have the absurdity of the above proposition any more exposed, than enough to have it rejected. I never heard or read any argument to prove the propriety of the disputed proposition. It is a begged proposition, and stands without the least shadow of evidence from Scripture or reason; but it requires no great ingenuity to see what the chimera was invented for; without it, the whole plan and scheme of atonement, which I am now examining, would fall for want of foundation.

There are some of Paul's writings to the Romans which have been used by divines to prove the partial plan of salvation true, of which I think it will be proper to take notice in this place. Romans ix. 21-22, has been made great use of in order to prove that God made some men vessels of eternal dishonor, and other vessels of eternal glory. The words read as follows:

Hath not the potter power over the clay, of the same lump to make one vessel unto honor, and another unto dishonor? What if God, willing to show his wrath, and to make his power known, endured with much long suffering the vessels of wrath fitted to destruction.

Again, Rom. xi. 7-10:

What then? Israel hath not obtained that which he seeketh; for but the election hath obtained it, and the rest were blinded (according as it is written, God hath given them the spirit of slumber, eyes that they should not see, and ears that they should not hear) unto this day. And David saith, let their table be made a snare, and a trap, and a stumbling block, and a recompense unto them; let their eyes be darkened, that they may not see, and bow down their back alway.

On this passage, and others like it, is built the doctrine of limited salvation by Jesus Christ, according to the foreknowledge and predestination of the Almighty. It is argued that those who are here called the elect are those for whom Christ died, and those alone who will finally obtain salvation by him. But why any person should make such a mistake in reading this chapter I am at a loss. The salvation of the elect is not argued in this chapter; but the certainty of the salvation of those who were blinded, and the propriety of believing it, occupies the greatest part of it.

Observe the words next to those we have quoted above, verse 11-12:

I say then, have they stumbled, that they should fall? God forbid: but rather through their fall salvation is come unto the Gentiles, to provoke them unto jealousy. Now, if the fall of them be the riches of the world, and the diminishing of them, the riches of the Gentiles, how much more their fullness?

Again, verse 15:

For if the casting away of them be the reconciling of the world, what shall the receiving of them be, but life from the dead?

Again, in his argument to the Romans he endeavors to show them, by the similitude of the branches of olive trees, that they ought to believe that those blinded ones, though broken off through unbelief, would be grafted in again. See verse 24:

> For, if thou wert cut out of the olive tree which is wild by nature, and wert grafted contrary to nature, into a good olive tree; how much more shall these, which be the natural branches, be grafted into their own olive tree?

The apostle seems desirous to instruct the Roman church, and argues the point fervently; see verses 25-26:

> For I would not, brethren, that ye should be ignorant of this mystery (lest ye should be wise in your own conceits), that blindness in part is happened to Israel, until the fullness of the Gentiles be come in. And so all Israel shall be saved; as it is written, there shall come out of Zion the Deliverer, and shall turn away ungodliness from Jacob.

Compare the last verse which I have quoted with Levit. xxvi. 44-45:

> And yet for all that, when they be in the land of their enemies, I will not cast them away, neither will I abhor them, to destroy them utterly, and to break my covenant with them: for I am the Lord their God. But I will for their sakes remember the covenant of their ancestors, whom I brought forth out of the land of Egypt, in the sight of the heathen that I might be their God: I am the Lord.

And Isaiah xiv. 25:

> In the Lord shall all the seed of Israel be justified, and shall glory.

Many like passages might be quoted from various parts of the scripture; but perhaps the above will suffice for this particular purpose. More of the like nature will be noticed in the sequel of this work.

The scriptures have been as much violated to maintain the doctrine which we are examining as good reason is by supposing God to be so infinitely partial, as he must be in the eye of reason in order to be what the doctrine represents him.

I shall now invite the attention of the reader to another system of atonement, which was undoubtedly formed with a view to shun the absurdities in the former, and to get rid of some of the consequences that were naturally deducible from that idea of the sufferings of Christ. This system supposes that the atonement by Christ was not intended for the salvation of any part of the human race; that its main end and sole object was the glory of the Supreme Being as manifested in his holy and righteous law. In support of this plan, it is argued that it is inconsistent for infinite wisdom and goodness to prefer an inferior object to a superior one; that all creation, when compared with the Creator, sinks into nothing, bearing no possible proportion to the infinite Jehovah; of course, that God always has his own glory in view as his supreme object in all he does.

This plan agrees with the former in supposing sin to be of infinite magnitude, and deserving of endless punishment; that, as the law of God is infinite, like himself, finite man is infinitely to blame for not fulfilling all its requirements; and that the penalty of the law is endless misery, which misery Christ sustained; not with a view of acquitting the sinner, nor in room and stead of the transgressor, as is supposed in the other plan; but for the honor of divine justice, and the glory of his Father. It is further argued that by Christ's suffering the penalty of the law, justice is as fully satisfied as if all mankind had been made miserable for an eternity. And this being the case it is now just and right for God to acquit as many of the sinful race of Adam as is consistent with his grand object, which is himself; yet by no means rendering it unjust for God to punish, to all eternity, as many as is necessary in order for the satisfying of the same grand object.

I first inquire into the propriety of the argument on which this plan of atonement seems to be founded; which is that God always acts for his own infinite and incomprehensible glory; never stooping so low as to act with an intention for the good of his creatures.

First: I ask is God as infinitely glorious as he can be, or not? If it be answered that he is, then if his object in all he does is to augment his own glory, he never has nor will he ever accomplish his intention. If it be argued that it is not to augment his own glory but to secure it and maintain it in its proper splendor, it argues it to be of a perishable nature, and that it would decay were it not for the continual vigilance of the Almighty in preserving it. If it be argued that neither of these objects is right, but that it is the manifestation of his glory to intelligent beings which is the grand design or object of God in all his acts without any reference to the effect which this manifestation has on those to whom it is made, I say the object has now dwindled into annihilation; there is not the smallest imaginable atom of it left. To suppose that any rational being can wish or desire to accomplish any piece of labor without having any reference to the consequences, is too glaringly absurd to need refutation.

Now the nature of the proposition which I am examining confines the motive of Deity within himself, and himself from his creation. In order, therefore, to look at the Almighty as he is by this doctrine represented, we must look at him as destitute of a creation, and view him abstractly from all his creatures. But may I ask, what title to give that being of whom we speak? The name *Jehovah* truly has reference to his self-existence, and to his character as the giver of existence also. The name *God* implies a being who is worshipped. *Lord* signifies a possessor. "*I am that I am*" has reference to an unchangeable being, but does not determine a being of goodness.

I ask again, what do we know of an Almighty, only by his works? If his existence can ever be determined by any other means, I am ignorant of the way. What do we know but by our senses? Have we any sense of good or evil that does not concern created beings? We may say, if we please, that God acts for his own essential good abstractly from his creation; but what do we mean by it? An action for the good of any being, presupposes that being in want; and if in want, then not infinitely happy. If God be not infinitely happy, he never can be. I inquire further, by what data can we determine that God is a good being? Can we determine it by any other criterion than by the effects of what he does, as it concerns his creatures? The truth undoubtedly is that just as far as we can look into creation, providence, and redemption, and see the harmony and beauty of them, and see that all were calculated for the good of created intelligences, whom these things concern, we are satisfied that he who conducts the whole is a good being. And if we say he is good, without this understanding, we acknowledge a proposition for which we are unable to offer the smallest reason.

Again, is it not wrong to make a separation where the Almighty does not? Is he not perfectly joined to his creation? Do we not live, move, and have our being in God? Were we not created of his fullness? Had Deity anything of which to create beings but his own eternal nature? I know it has been said that God created all things out of nothing, etc.; but such an idea never will be imbibed by me until I can form, in imagination at least, a notion of how much nothing it takes to make the least imaginable something. If all things were created of the infinite Jehovah, as great a part of his creation as we take from him, so great a proportion we take from his fullness. God never could be more than infinite in his fullness; then, to take the smallest creature from him, which he created of that infinite fullness, you have left something less than infinity. Now, if it be argued that God acts for the good of himself, considering his creatures to belong to his fullness, I am perfectly agreed; but to say that the Almighty has, or ever could have a motive in action that did not embrace every consequence that could arise from what he did, would be limiting his omnisciency; or to say that he did not intend good to all whom his acts concern, would be limiting his goodness and would be an impeachment on his justice.

I have before in this work contended that all the attributes which we ascribe to God we call good, on account of the advantages which we derive from such principles. We are told of a

God who acts for his own benefit abstractly from his creation; and that in millions of cases he finds it most for his glory to make his rational, hoping, wanting creatures endlessly miserable; and this is called goodness. We are likewise told of a devil who acts for his own gratification, and who delights in making God's creatures miserable; and this is called badness. But for my part, according to such statements, the difference between goodness and badness is so small I can hardly distinguish it. It is profane, in my opinion, to attribute a disposition to the Almighty which we can justly condemn in ourselves. A man who should act from such a selfish principle as is attributed to God, would render himself wholly unworthy of the protection of common law. And shall we thus represent our kind and merciful Father, from whom ten thousand streams of goodness continually flow to his wanting and needy creatures? No; let every vibration of sense within us acknowledge his bountiful hand, which is never closed.

I have already labored in this work to show that sin is finite, and not committed against an infinite law. I shall, however, now call into examination a subject something like it, which is that of penalty; as it is contended that the penalty of God's law is endless punishment, etc.

I first inquire, why does a legislature affix penalties to laws which it makes? Answer: The first reason is: The strength and security of government. Second: That the punishment may serve to reclaim the delinquent. Third: That the punishment of a criminal may serve to deter others from the commission of like crimes. Fourth: In many cases, to keep the delinquent, by confinement or death, from doing any more mischief.

Now let us look into the government of an Almighty Being, and see how the matter of *penalty* will operate there. Observe the penalty is endless misery. I ask, is this necessary to secure the government of an Almighty Being? Would his government be in danger if this penalty were not enacted to his law? Supposing a legislature of men had the power in their hands of causing all the community on whom its laws were binding to love their laws in every requirement, and with vigilance to attend to the faithful discharge of their duties in all things, would it be necessary for them to enact penalties to their laws? Allowing the legislature to have such powers, who in the world would say it is not best to exercise it; that it is better to have penal laws, and let the people have their wicked, obdurate hearts, so that now and then we may have a poor criminal to execute? I can hardly believe that any will contend that penalty is necessary in the law of God in order to secure his government. Is there any scruple respecting God's power to turn the hearts of his creatures as he pleases? If there be not, then there is no need of a penalty in his law, in order for the security of his government.

Second: Is this penalty necessary, in order to reclaim the delinquent? Answer, that is impossible. The penalty being endless punishment, it can have no object in reclaiming the punished. The execution of such a penalty on any of God's creatures would prove the contractedness of his goodness, as no possible good could be communicated to a victim of such punishment. Divine truths says, God is good unto all, and his tender mercies are over all his works. To say God is good to a creature of his whom he irrevocably dooms to endless torments is a violation of our senses; and no person, in a moment of sobriety, will believe it. It is then evident that such a penalty would not be necessary to reclaim the sinner.

Third: Is it necessary to inflict such a penalty on the transgressor in order to deter others from the commission of sin? Answer, no; for, according to the doctrine which I am examining, the first transgression committed involved the whole human race in the delinquency; and an execution of such a penalty would be the endless misery of the whole family of man; there would not have been one left to be deterred from sinning, or even to tell the news!

Fourth: Is such a penalty necessary in order to keep the sinner from sinning any more? So far from that, this penalty would fix the delinquents in a situation in which they could do nothing but sin, to an endless eternity. No moral being can be miserable as suffering conscious guilt, without sin; therefore, in order for endless misery to be inflicted, endless transgression is necessary.

Look, kind reader, and see what an absurdity lies here. Because a being has sinned once, the law which he violated requires that he should continue in transgression! Well, he complies; will the law justify him? But, says the reader, I do not understand you. Why, the matter is plain; if a moral being cannot be miserable without sin, he must continue in sin in order to be miserable. Then if God's law requires endless misery, it requires endless transgression! But, it is argued, a law cannot exist without a penalty. This undoubtedly is an error. The largest signification of the word law *is* governing power. See Rom. vii. 23:

> But I see another law in my members, warring against the law of my mind, and bringing me into captivity unto the law of sin which is in my members.

This law of sin in the members, which brings the man into captivity, is undoubtedly the power of the flesh, which lusteth against the spirit, that we cannot do the things we would. Now, I ask, is there any penalty to this law? Does this law administer any condemnation to those who do not obey it? Most surely it does not. Then pass to the eighth chapter and third verse:

> For the law of the spirit of life in Christ Jesus hath made me free from the law of sin and death.

This law is undoubtedly the governing power of the new man which overcomes the carnal mind, and delivers the soul from the bondage of sin. I ask, again, is there any penalty to this law? Is there a dispensation of condemnation administered by this law of life? Truth says, the wages of sin is death.

Does this death flow from the law of the spirit of life in Christ Jesus? Surely not. "To be carnally minded is death." (Rom. viii. 6.)

If carnal mindedness be that death, which is the wages of sin, surely it does not flow from the spirit of life. "To be spiritually minded is life and peace." (Rom. viii. 6.)

God's moral law is like himself, love: "God is love, and he who loveth, dwelleth in God, and God in him." (1 John iv. 16.)*

It requires all moral beings to love God and each other; and the reason why it commands this is,— it is love itself. True, that soul is miserable that does not love God; and the reasons are, love is the life and happiness of the soul, and hatred is its death and misery.

Although I think I have given unanswerable reasons why I do not admit such a penalty as we have examined, I will for the sake of the argument still further allow it, and inquire into Christ's suffering it.

To say that Christ has suffered such a penalty is a contradiction in terms, because endless duration has not yet expired. To say that this penalty ever will be suffered by Christ, or any other being, is another contradiction in words; for an endless duration will never expire. Then to say that such a penalty has been, or ever will be, suffered, is erroneous.

If it be argued that Christ was an infinite person, and, therefore, could suffer an endless punishment in a few moments; we answer, it is not shunning the contradiction. If the position be moved, and the argument is that he, being infinite, could suffer as much in a few moments as all mankind would to an endless duration; I ask, are there more infinite beings than one? All answer, no. I ask again, is it possible for that infinite being to suffer? Even from my opponent, the answer will be that an infinite being did not suffer; but that it was the finite nature which suffered and was raised from the dead by the infinite; that it was the human nature which was made a sin offering; and that the divine nature gave

---

* The actual wording of this key passage for Universalists: "God is love; and he that dwelleth in love dwelleth in God, and God in him." —Editor.

victory to the human by raising it into an immortal life. Well then, the sufferings were finite, and could by no means answer the requirements of an infinite penalty.

The particular difference between this plan and the former is in the intentions of the sufferings of Christ. The former supposes that Christ suffered in room and in stead of the sinner, so as to acquit all those from condemnation for whom he died:— This argues, that the intention of the sufferings of Christ was not the salvation of sinners but, as we have before observed, the glory of the Supreme Being; but that by the sufferings of Christ the law is perfectly magnified, and made honorable; and that it is just for God to acquit as many of the sinful race of Adam as is consistent with his glory; but does not render it unjust for him to punish, endlessly, as many as is necessary for the same grand object.

Now, admitting the penalty of the law to be endless, and that Christ suffered it in full, the law cannot now require the destruction of the offender; how then can we reasonably argue, that it is for the glory of God to punish, when justice does not require it? If justice does require it now of any, it does of all. If it be argued that divine justice does not require the endless happiness or misery of man, we say it is not a law which concerns mankind; and if we say God's will, in the misery of mankind, extends farther than the requirements of his justice, it is setting the Almighty against himself. Again, admitting such provisions to be made as render it consistent with justice, that all sinners should be emancipated from death and misery, does eternal love and mercy require less?

Supposing five hundred Americans are in slavery at Algiers. Our Consul demands the price of their redemption, per man; he is answered, the price of one is the price of the whole; and the price of the whole is the price of one; the sum is five hundred dollars. This, the Dey says, is not a consideration for the slaves, but to show America, or the United states, his power, and the dignity of his government. Our consul obtains the money and pays it. Now, reader, do you think he would confine the benefits of this ransom-money to a small part of those unfortunate Americans; and out of five hundred, send but fifty home to their wives, children, country and friends; and tell the remaining four hundred and fifty that the money was his own, and he had a right to extend, or not extend the benefits of it, as he pleased; and that it was his pleasure that they should all wear out a miserable life in slavery, where they might dream of liberty but never enjoy it? The smallest degree of humanity would argue better things.

We have now examined the foundation of this plan of atonement, and it has removed out of our sight; we have sought carefully after the penalty of the law, and cannot find it; we have sought for the satisfaction of such penal requirements, admitting they did exist, and find them not; we have admitted, for the sake of the query, that such satisfaction did take place, and we have sought for the consequences which are argued, and find them inconsistent with such promises.

Taking my leave of this plan of atonement, I shall introduce a third one; from which I shall also dissent, and give my reasons for so doing. The plan agrees with the former in respect to the law, its penalty and of the personage of him who makes the atonement; but differs, in respect to the *intentions* of God in the atonement.

As far as the first transgression concerned mankind, it is believed that the atonement by Christ is fully efficacious; and that no man will, or can be, miserable forever on account of what is called original sin. And that, by virtue of the sufferings of Christ, Adam and all his posterity were immediately placed in a state of trial, or probation, after the fall; such as Adam was in before, but with this difference, viz., man now knows good and evil, and is possessed of strong appetites to sin; but has also a portion of the divine Spirit, which is given to every man for his profit to assist him in opposing those appetites and subduing them.

Those who believe in this plan believe that it was in the power of Adam, as a moral agent, to have stood in a state of holiness and innocence; and that it is now in the power of every man, as a moral agent, to obtain the paradise which Adam lost. They do not admit that Christ died for our actual transgressions, after we come to years of discretion; but of these we must repent, and beg for mercy, and God will forgive, on our humble and sincere application. The sum of this plan of atonement made salvation *possible* unto all men but *certain* unto none. It argues that it is the will of God that all men should be saved, and come unto the knowledge of the truth; that all should repent of their sins, and receive the Redeemer on the reasonable terms upon which he is offered to us.

Those who believe in this plan believe it possible for men to neglect those privileges, slight those merciful offers, and turn a deaf ear to all the warnings of the Spirit, until the day of their probation is ended; whereby all that the Savior has done is made of no effect unto them. And that thousands will be thus neglectful and be miserable as long as God exists, not, however, for the sin which Adam committed, but for their own personal transgressions.

Before I put the foregoing system of atonement under examination, I will take notice of the character of the Mediator, as believed in by all those who hold to the several systems of which we have taken notice; as I have not examined that particular in my inquiries on the other systems preceding the one under consideration. They all contend that the Mediator is really God; that the Godhead consists of three distinct persons, viz., Father, Son and Holy Ghost; that these distinct persons are equal in power and glory, and eternally and essentially one.

The reader will observe my usual mode of reasoning, which is to admit, as truth, what I wish to oppose; and to oppose it with the consequence which necessarily follows. For the sake of argument, then, I admit the foregoing statement concerning Christ to be just; and then we contend, that if he be the *Son of God*, he is the *son of himself*, and is his own father; that he is no more the Son of God, than God is his son!

To say of two persons, exactly of the same age, that one of them is a real son of the other, is to confound good sense. If Jesus Christ were really God, it must be argued that God really died! Again, if the Godhead consists of three distinct persons, and each of those persons be infinite, the whole Godhead amounts to the amazing sum of infinity, multiplied by three! If it is said that neither of these three persons alone is infinite, we say the three together, with the addition of a million more such, would not make an infinite being. But supposing we get over all those absurdities, and suppose that these three distinct persons formed the grand council in heaven, on the salvation of man, after the first transgression.

In this council, and on so momentous an occasion, the first person addresses the other two, saying: The colony which we have just planted on our new-made earth has rebelled; and you know the penalty, which is endless misery, must be immediately executed on the two delinquents, unless a dispensation can be devised more favorable to the offenders, and equally satisfactory to justice. As the attribute of justice spake in the first person, that of mercy speaks in the second, and proposes a pardon. Justice opposes, and contends that his honor depends on the penalty's being put in execution. Mercy again replies, the second person in the Godhead shall suffer the penalty due to sin, and justice shall grant man a second probation in which he may secure the life, which he, by rebellion, lost. That reasonable conditions should be proposed, and the third person should make them known to man, and give him proper directions how to fulfill them; and if man faithfully attend to these conditions, he secures his happiness; if not, mercy makes no more request in favor of the offender. To this all agree; and it is registered accordingly.

It seems according to this plan that man utterly failed on the first trial, but now has the second opportunity. I would ask, is there any more certainty of his succeeding now than there was before? Is it certain, according to this plan, that any of Adam's posterity will obtain salvation? Is it not in the power of all men to neglect those conditions? If it be not, it destroys the nature of conditions, and of probation; if it be, then it is entirely uncertain, whether an individual soul will ever be saved by the Gospel plan.

I have before shown it erroneous to suppose that any finite being could suffer an infinite punishment, in any period of time; and I think it is also granted that an infinite being cannot suffer. But admitting the system of atonement to stand on the ground contended for, it was a matter of utter uncertainty whether it would, in any instance, prove efficacious as it respected the salvation of man.

A rich parent gives a large portion to his son, accompanied with good advice; the son turns prodigal, spends all, and gets into prison for debt. The father still loves the son, pays his debts, lets him out of prison, sets him at liberty, and gives him a thousand pounds more, which is all he ever can give him, and tells him to be more prudent. The prodigal, no sooner than he finds himself thus liberated, and in possession of a handsome property, goes into the same error which brought him to ruin before, and finally meets the same consequences. The father has no more to give, and the son becomes a vagabond. We ask, did the parent act the part of wisdom any more than the son did? If he had acted wisely, would he not have said to him: Son, I gave you much at the first; I gave you good advice; I told you that industry and prudence alone would secure you from want; I told you, though your property were large, unless you put your money to interest, or into trade, it must dwindle; that if you threw away your time in vain and foolish prodigality, the end would be what you have already experienced? And although I hoped better things of you than a total neglect of my admonitions, yet so I feared; and, for your good, have reserved one thousand pounds of what I intended to give you, which, had you been economical, I should by this time have committed to your care. But as you have conducted so foolishly, I must, for your benefit, keep the remainder of your portion, until you prove yourself a convert from prodigality to economy.

If the Almighty were ignorant, at first, when he put man in possession of privileges which he afterwards abused, it astonishes me that he should risk the last favor which he had to bestow on principles which he had just seen fail. It will undoubtedly be acknowledged by all that Jehovah knew, as perfectly before transgression as afterward, what man would do, and how he would dispose of the advantages which he had bestowed on him. Then, I ask, if God knew how man would abuse those privileges, and knew he would be eternally miserable in consequence, was it an act of kindness in God to grant man such privileges? I ask again, was it possible for that to fail which the Almighty perfectly knew would take place? The answer will be, no. Then, when we have consolidated the whole down to its real self, all the privilege which God gave to those whom he knew would render themselves objects of his displeasure was a privilege of incurring to themselves endless misery; I say more, he insured it to them himself by putting that into their hands, by which he knew it would be effected.

I give my child a loaded pistol, which I tell him to discharge at a serpent on his way where I have ordered him. I know perfectly well when I give him the pistol that he will carelessly blow his own brains out with its contents, and the serpent will go unhurt; the child's end happens accordingly. I leave the reader to judge whether I am the murderer of my child; my conscience would inform me so.

The Mediator suffered the penalty of the law to reinstate man in a state of probation; God made a revelation to mankind for their instruction; he inspired the ancient prophets to speak of the things of his kingdom; sent his holy Spirit into the world to lead and guide man into all truth; and all this is done from the pure benevolence of God towards a sinful world, for its everlasting welfare, but all upon uncertainties! After all, man has it in his power to frustrate the whole plan of grace, and render it abortive!

On the other hand, it was possible for every son and daughter of Adam to accept of Christ on the very easy terms of Gospel obedience, and thereby to have secured the heavenly kingdom. This being granted, who knows they will not do it? Things that are possible, may be done; and who can say, for certainty, that those things which are possible will not be effected? If it be an absolute certainty that any will finally fail of gaining the prize, it is also an absolute certainty that they have no possible opportunity for it: — If there be an opportunity, and the prize be attainable by all, there is at least some room for hope; and were it the real Christian hope, it would be like an anchor to the soul, both sure and steadfast; but being founded in the creature, and not in God, it is wavering and doubtful.

On this system, it must be absurd to argue the certainty of the endless misery of any of the family of man, as the salvation of the whole is possible. God, out of love to his creatures, made it possible for them all to obtain salvation; indeed, it is his will that all should be saved from their sins; it is also the will of Christ, and of the Holy Spirit; it is the will of all holy beings in heaven, and of the saints on earth; prayers are daily offered up from the altar of sacrifice for its accomplishment. And if it be not done, the whole Godhead will be disappointed; mourning, instead of rejoicing, will be the employment of holy angels; and the saints will be stung with the keenest sensations of grief.

No one will dare to say he believes God can be disappointed in any of his purposes; therefore, those who believe in the system last examined must be dissatisfied with it, if their eyes should ever be opened to see its consequences.

Having examined those several systems of atonement, in as concise a method as was convenient, and having given my principal reasons for not adopting either, I now beg the attention of the reader to my second inquiry, viz. the necessity of atonement, and where satisfaction must be made.

5. The Necessity of Atonement, and Where Satisfaction Must Be Made

I have already entered my protest against the necessity of atonement, on the principles upon which Christians have generally believed it, by showing the finite nature of sin, and the error of supposing that the law of God required the endless misery of mankind as a penal requisition.

Atonement signifies reconciliation, or satisfaction, which is the same. It is a state of being unreconciled to truth and justice which needs reconciliation; and it is a state of dissatisfied being which needs satisfaction. Therefore I raise my inquiry on the question: Is *God* the unreconciled or dissatisfied party, or is it *man*?

For our assistance on this question, let us turn our attention to God's dealings with Adam on the day of transgression, and the conduct of Adam, the transgressor. After Adam had eaten of the forbidden fruit, his eyes opened to the knowledge of good and evil, and he found himself naked, and endeavored to hide himself from God, which he certainly would not have done had he considered his Maker his friend. Sin produced two errors in the mind of Adam which have been very incident to mankind ever since; the first was he believed God to be his enemy, in consequence of disobedience; and secondly, that he could reconcile his Maker by works of his own. The first of these errors we discover from Adam's endeavoring to hide from God; and the second is seen in his endeavoring to clothe himself with the works of his own hands.

It is plain that a material change had taken place in Adam; but can we prove that any alteration happened in God? It is very evident that Adam was unreconciled to God; but it is equally as evident that God was not unreconciled to him. God's calling Adam in the cool of the day, and asking him where he was; clothing him with a garment of skins, and promising that the seed of the woman should bruise the serpent's head, are beautiful representations of the parental love and fatherly care of the Creator. It ought to be observed that God pronounced no curse on Adam, but on the serpent. If the Almighty had been unreconciled or dissatisfied with his creature man, in room of promising him a final victory over the serpent, the curse would undoubtedly have fallen on the object of his displeasure.

To say that God loved man any less after transgression than before, denies his unchangeability; but to say that man was wanting in love to God, places him in his real character. As God was not the unreconciled party, no atonement was necessary for his reconciliation. Where there is dissatisfaction, it presupposes an injured party; and can it be hard to determine which was injured by sin, the Creator or the sinner? If God were unreconciled to man, the atonement was necessary to renew his love to his creature; but if man were the unreconciled, the atonement was necessary to renew his love to his Creator. The matter is now stated so plainly that no person who can read can mistake.

I shall now endeavor to prove from scripture that the atonement by Christ was the effect and not the cause of God's love to man. See St. John iii. 16:

> For God so loved the world that he gave his only begotten Son, that whosoever believeth on him might no perish, but have everlasting life.

According to this passage, nothing is more plain in Scripture than the idea that what Christ did for sinners was a consequence of God's love to them. Again, verse 17:

> for God sent not his Son into the world to condemn the world, but that the world through him might be saved.

This passage says that God did not send his Son into the world to condemn the world; but according to the general idea of the atonement, Christ stood as the *proxy of man*, and the world was tried in him, and condemned in him, and in him suffered the penalty of the law which man had transgressed. It is also said, in the text, that Christ was sent that the world through him might be saved; which, if true, goes to prove that the Father's object in Christ's coming into the world was the salvation of the sinner, and not for the removing of any dissatisfaction in himself towards them. Again, see Rom. v. 8:

> But God commendeth his love towards us in that while we were yet sinners, Christ dies for us.

As the death of Christ is here spoken of as a commendation of God's love to us, it ought to be considered as an effect and not the cause of that love. Again, 1st Epistle of John iv. 9:

> In this was manifested the love of God towards us, because that God sent his only begotten Son into the world that we might live through him.

If Christ's coming into the world were a manifestation of God's love to us, this love must have existed before he came, and his coming was an effect produced by it. Verse 10: "Herein is love, not that we loved God, but that he loved us, and sent his son to be the propitiation for our sins." Verse 19: "We love him because he first loved us."

From those passages, and many more which might be quoted to the same effect, it is easy to learn that what the Mediator did for sinners was the consequence and not the cause of God's love to us. God being infinite in all his glorious attributes, he can by no means love at one time and hate the same object at another. His divine omniscience comprehended all the events of time and eternity; therefore nothing could take place to remove his love from an object on which it was placed. The Almighty had no occasion to dislike Adam after transgression, any more than he had even before he made him; for he knew as well then that Adam would sin, as he did after it was actually done. The reason that we mortals love an object at one time, and dislike it another, is the weakness of our understandings; we have not always the same view of the same object. We may slight an object of great value, its excellence being out of our sight; and we may set our affections on one of no value by erroneously attaching a value to it which it did not possess. But the Infinitely Wise is subject to no mistakes; he comprehends the whole futurition of all moral beings, and loves them as his own offspring, with a love consistent with his immutable existence. Therefore, it is evident, that God was not the unreconciled, and, of course, did not require an atonement to reconcile himself to his creatures.

Let us now turn on the other side, and see if man be not reconciled to God; and if it would not be more reasonable to reconcile man to his Maker than to reconcile God to the sinner. See Psalm xiv. 2-3:

> The Lord looked down from heaven upon the children of men, to see if there were any that did understand and seek God. They are all gone aside; they are altogether become filthy: there is none that doeth good, no, not one.

The apostle Paul, in the third chapter of Romans, giving a general description of mankind, introduces it with the passage from Psalms, which I have just quoted, and continues it by an assemblage of various passages (verses 13-18):

> Their throat is an open sepulcher; with their tongues they have used deceit; the poison of asps is under their lips; whose mouth is full of cursing and bitterness; their feet are swift to shed blood; destruction and misery are in their ways; and the way of peace they have not known; there is no fear of God before their eyes.

It is very evident that the apostle meant to exclude none from this description, as the reader may learn from verse 19:

> Now we know, that what thing soever the law saith, it saith to them who are under the law; that every mouth may be stopped, and all the world may become guilty before God.

Again, chap. v. 12:

> Wherefore, as by one man, sin entered into the world, and death by sin, and do death passed upon all men, for that all have sinned.

That the scriptures abundantly prove that all men are sinners, and in an unreconciled state, will not be disputed by any. Then it is certainly man that needs reconciliation. Men, while dictated by a carnal mind, are dissatisfied with God; they accuse him of being a hard master, reaping where he has not sown, and gathering where he has not strewed. They think on the Almighty, but desire not the knowledge of his ways. They behold no beauty in him; he appears as a tyrant, regardless of his creatures. A consciousness of sin, without the knowledge of God, represents Deity as angry and full of vengeance; in which sense, many Scriptures are written, as I have before observed. How often do we find that God has been provoked to wrath and jealousy, and his fury raised to a flame against the sinner? And how often do the scriptures represent him repenting of his anger, and growing calm!

All these scriptures are written according to the circumstances of the creature, and the apprehensions which the unreconciled entertain of God. Viewing man in this state of unreconciliation to God and holiness, it appears evidently necessary that he should receive an atonement productive of a renewal of love to his Maker. Without atonement, God could never be seen as he is, "altogether lovely... and the chiefest among ten thousand" (Song of Sol. v. 16, 10); nor could he be loved with the whole heart, mind, might and strength. How often are men displeased at the Supreme Being himself? What an infinite number of hard speeches have sinners spoken against God? All which argue the necessity of atonement, whereby those maladies may be healed.

What an infinite difference there is between the All-gracious and Merciful, and his lost and bewildered creatures? He, all glorious, without a spot in the whole infinitude of his nature; all lovely, without exception, and loving, without partiality. Who can tell the thousandth part of his love to his offspring? And this invariably the same through every dispensation, without the smallest abatement. But what can we say of man? Lost in a wilderness of sin, wandering in the by-paths of iniquity, lost to the knowledge of his heavenly Benefactor, and dissatisfied with his God; he goes on grumbling and complaining, attributing the worst of characters to the most merciful, and entertaining no regard for the fountain of all his comforts. God never called for a sacrifice to reconcile himself to man; but loved man so infinitely, that he was pleased to bruise his Son for our own good, to give him to die, in attestation of love to sinners.

The belief that the great Jehovah was offended with his creatures to such a degree that nothing but the death of Christ or the endless misery of mankind could appease his anger, is an idea that has done more injury to the Christian religion than the writings of all its opposers for many centuries. The error has been fatal to the life and spirit of the religion of Christ in our world; all those principles which are to be dreaded by men, have been believed to exist in God; and professors have been molded into the image of their Deity, and become more cruel than the uncultivated savage! A persecuting inquisition is a lively representation of the God which professed Christians have believed in ever since the apostasy. It is every day's practice to represent the Almighty so offended with man, that he employs his infinite mind in devising unspeakable tortures, as retaliations on those with whom he is offended. Those ideas have so obscured the whole nature of God from us, that the capacious religion of the human mind has been darkened by the almost impenetrable cloud; even the tender charities of nature have been frozen with such tenets, and the natural friendship common to human society, has, in a thousand instances, been driven from the walks of man.

But, says the reader, is it likely that persecution ever rose from men's believing, that God was an enemy to wicked man? Undoubtedly; for had all professors of Christianity believed that God had compassion on the ignorant and those who are out of the way, how could they have persecuted those whom they believe in error? But, with contrary views, whose who professed to believe in Christ, who professed to be the real disciples of him who taught his disciples to love their enemies, have been the fomenters of persecution; they have persecuted even unto death, those who could not believe all the absurdities in orthodox creeds. It may be asked, if those animosities did not arise from pride, ambition, and carnal mindedness? I answer, yes; and so does the God in whom persecuting Christians believe, for they form a God altogether like unto themselves; therefore, while they vainly fancy they are in the service of the true God, they are following the dictates of pride and unlawful ambition, the natural production of a carnal mind; and atonement is the only remedy for the evil.

Men are dissatisfied with the Almighty and his providence; they are dissatisfied with, and are enemies of, one another; whereas our true happiness consists of loving God, and our neighbors. Men in possession of vile appetites, pursue with greediness, their gratification; but still, they retain their wants, their souls are allied to heaven and holiness, and can never be happy without them. They are conscious of sin, and feel condemnation resting on their minds; they look forward to the awful scene of dissolution, and their souls start back with horror. Death is the king of terrors to the unreconciled; how awful are the thoughts of death to those whose hopes are only the feeble productions of their fears and wants, unsupported with divine evidence! Oh, how necessary is atoning grace on such an occasion, whereby a divine confidence may by enjoyed; the value thereof cannot be estimated by earthly treasures; all the shining dust of India, and the riches of the south, are poverty when compared with the riches of a reconciled mind.

Without atonement, God's glorious design in the everlasting welfare of his offspring, man, could never be effected; the ordination of an infinitely merciful God could never be carried into effect. The Almighty must not be deprived of the means of accomplishing his gracious designs. We read of his covenant with day and night, which cannot be broken; but it would be broken at once, should the causes cease that produce their changes. So of the covenant of eternal mercy, the testament of eternal life, it must be put in force by the death of the testator, and its life and immortal glory be brought to light through his resurrection. Let it be understood, that it is man who receives the atonement, who stands in need of reconciliation, who, being dissatisfied, needs satisfaction; and not place those imperfections and wants in him who is infinite in his fullness; and the doctrine of atonement may be sought for in the nature of things, and found to be rational to the understanding.

That man receives the atonement, was evidently the opinion of St. Paul (see Rom. v. 11):

> And not only so, but we also joy in God, through our Lord Jesus Christ, by whom we have now received the atonement.

Were there a single passage in the Scriptures that would reach half as far in proving that God received the atonement as the one just quoted does to prove that man received it, the matter might be considered more disputable than it now is.

We read that men are enemies to God by wicked works, which teaches us that enmity is wickedness. Should we then dare to say that God is our enemy? It is wrong for us to be enemies even to those who injure us, much more to those who never had it is their power to do us any harm. I wish to ask, did any of God's creatures ever injure him? Surely not. Why then does he turn our enemy? He commands us to love our enemies, that we may be like him; but if he hate his enemies, we must hate ours if we would be like him. If he be not our enemy, he needs no atonement. But if men are enemies to God, they need an atonement to bring them to love him who loves them.

Here the reader will observe that we shun those difficulties which have represented the Gospel of Christ so inconsistent. We now view the Almighty the same, yesterday, today, and forever; by no means changed in his disposition towards his creatures, but always designing and working in all things, for their good. Here is no need of the self-contradictory notion of altering an unalterable being; of satisfying an infinite dissatisfaction; of reconciling a being who was never unreconciled; of producing love in love itself; of causing an eternal unchangeable friend to be friendly, or of offering a sacrifice to the eternal father of our spirits, to cause him to love and have mercy on his offspring.

How much more reasonable it is to suppose ourselves in need of those alterations. But unhappily men have looked at Deity through the medium of a carnal mind, and have formed all their evil tempers in Jehovah; like the deceived astronomer, who fancied he saw a monster in the sun, occasioned by a fly on his glass. The creature being in the medium of sight, was supposed to be in the object beheld; and though it was small in itself, and would have appeared so, could it have been seen where it was; yet carrying it into the sun, it magnified to an enormous size. So it is with our vile and sinful passions, could we behold them in ourselves, and view them as they are, they would appear in their finite and limited sphere; but the moment we form those passions in Deity, they magnify to infinity. Let a council of astronomers be called who are all deceived by the fly; let them consult on the bigness of the monster, calculate how long it has been growing, and how soon it may wholly absorb the sun; let them endeavor to account for its cause, and analyze its constitution, inform us of the degrees of heat its lungs sustain, and how many degrees hotter it is than iron can be heated in a furnace. But here is room for disagreement, which may give rise to great disputations. To one, it appears much larger than to another; they cannot judge alike, with regard to its age, nor how much larger it will grow; some are ready to dispute its being a living creature, fancying it may be an opaque body. They are all agreed that there is a phenomenon in the sun, but dispute, and even quarrel, about its peculiarities. What would become of all their calculations the moment they should discover the fly? All would be gone, at once, and the sun would be relieved of the burden of so ponderous a monster.

How many various calculations have divines made, on the *fury* and *wrath* which they have discovered in God. How much they have preached and written, on the awful subject; and how many the ways they have invented, to appease such wrath and vengeance! When we come to see the error, and find those principles in ourselves, all those notions vanish at once. The fly on the glass might easily have been removed, or destroyed; but had there been a monster in the sun, what calculations could mortals have made to remove it; enmity in man may be overcome with love; but, did it exist in God, it must be infinite and eternal.

To conclude, the supposition that Deity receives the atonement, or any possible advantage from the Gospel plan whereby an alteration is effected in him for the better, amounts to the inexplicable absurdity of making omniscience more wise, omnipotence more powerful, justice more just; and of giving love the power of loving, of making mercy more merciful, truth more true, and goodness better; for these are the seven spirits of God, which are in all the earth, and they are without the shadow of turning.

Having shown, as I hope, to the reader's satisfaction, the necessity of atonement, and where satisfaction must be made and reconciliation take place, I shall pass to make some inquires into the personage of the Mediator who makes the atonement, and his ability for performing the work.

6. The Personage and Character of the Mediator

I have already stated some of the absurdities contained in the opinions of most Christians, respecting the mediator; we shall now be a little more particular on the subject.

I shall contend that the Mediator is a created dependent being. That he is a created being is proved from Rev. iii. 14, where he is said to be "the beginning of the creation of God." His dependency is proved by his frequent prayers to the Father. That he acknowledged a superior, when on earth, is evident from many passages which might be quoted. See. St. John v. 19; Christ here says:

> The Son can do nothing of himself, but what he seeth the Father do.

He acknowledged a superior in knowledge; see Matt. xxiv. 36:

> But of that day and hour knoweth no man, no, not the angels in heaven, but my Father only.

This passage implies, that he did not know of that day himself. St. Mark is still more explicit; see chap. xiii. 32:

> But of that day and that hour knoweth no man, no, not the angels which are in heaven, neither the Son, but the Father.

And further, that he acknowledges a superior, even in his risen glory, may be proved from his own words to his servant John, on the Isle of Patmos; see Rev. iii. 12:

> Him that overcometh, will I make a pillar in the temple of my God, and he shall go no more out; and I will write upon him the name of my God, and the name of the city of my God, which is new Jerusalem, which cometh down out of heaven from my God, and I will write upon him my new name.

Four times, in the above passage, he acknowledges a being whom he worships. Again, see Psalm xlv. 7:

> Thou lovest righteousness and hatest wickedness, because God,

thy God hath anointed thee with the oil of gladness above thy fellows.

The reader will observe, I have ventured to put the word "because" in place of the word "therefore" in this quotation; but we have not done it without the authority of a former translation. The difference is so essential, I cannot dispense with it. Observe, the writer of the Psalm addresses one God, and speaks in his address of another, see verse 6, "Thy throne, O God, is forever and ever." This God is dependant on another, expressed in verse 7, "because God, thy God hath anointed thee," etc.

That the names "God," "Lord," and "everlasting Father" are applied to Christ, I shall not dispute; neither shall I dispute the propriety of it; but I do not admit that they mean the self-existent Jehovah, when applied to the Mediator. In the quotation from the Psalm, Christ is said to be anointed above his fellows. Fellows are equals. Who are Christ's equals? Perhaps the reader may say, they are the Father and the Holy Spirit; but I can hardly believe that Christ was anointed with the oil of gladness above his Father, neither do I believe any one will contend for it. I am sensible that God speaks by the prophet of smiting the man who is his fellow; but this fellowship must be different from the one just spoken of, and stands only in an official sense. The reader will then ask if I would consider the Mediator no more than equal with men? I answer, yes, were it not that our Father and his Father, our God and his God, hath anointed him above his fellows. See Philippians ii. 9:

> Wherefore God also hath highly exalted him, and given him a name which is above every name.

For this exaltation and name, he was dependant on his Father, and received them from him. This name, which is above every name, is the name of God, named on Jesus.

It will be said, Christ taught the people, that he and his Father were one. I grant he did, and if that prove him to be essentially God, the argument must run farther than the objector would wish to have it; see St. John xvii. 11. Christ prays that his disciples may be one, even as he and the Father are one. The oneness of the Father and Son is their union and agreement in the great work which he has undertaken; and he prayed that his disciples might be as well agreed in the Gospel of salvation, as he and his Father were, see verse 18: "As thou hast sent me into the world, so have I also sent them into the world." The Father of all mercies sent his Son Jesus into the world, for a certain purpose; and there was a perfect agreement between them, in all things. He says, he came not to do his own will, but the will of him who sent him. And again, My meat and drink, is to do the will of him who sent me, and to finish his work.

The President of the United States sends a minister to negotiate a peace at a foreign court; this minister must conduct according to the authority which he derives from him by whom he is sent; and as far as he does, he is, in his official character, the power that sent him. It is evident Christ received the power which he exercises in the work which he hath undertaken, and that his kingdom was given to him, which goes to prove he did not eternally possess them; see Dan. vii. 14: "And there was given him dominion and glory, and a kingdom." According to the prophecy here quoted, the dominion, glory, and kingdom of Christ were given him. The people whom he is to rule are given him, see Psalm ii. 8:

> Ask of me, and I shall give the heathen for thine inheritance,
> and the uttermost parts of the earth for thy possession.

St. Matthew xxviii. 18; Jesus saith: "All power is given unto me in heaven and earth." Chap. xi. 27: "All things are delivered unto me of my Father." These and many more passages are found in sacred writ, in support of the dependence of the Mediator on the Supreme Eternal, and that he derives his power and glory from him. But if Christ be essentially God, all those scriptures seem without just signification.

It is written, that man was created in the image of God; and, by the light of the Gospel, St. Paul ventured to assert that Christ is this image. The reader will do well to observe that the image of a person, and the person, are not essentially one, but some knowledge of a person may be obtained by his true image. Christ being the image of God, it is by him we learn the nature of the Father. Christ saith, "No man knoweth the Father but the Son,... and he to whom the Son revealeth him." (Matt. x. 27.) Again, "No man cometh unto the Father, but by me." (John xiv. 6.) St. Paul is particular on this subject in his 1st Epistle to Timothy, see chap. ii. verse 5: "For there is one God, and one Mediator between God and men, the man Christ Jesus." It seems by this testimony that St. Paul was a stranger to the notion of Christ's being essentially God, as it would be improper to call him a man were that the case. If it be argued that Christ is God and man both, I ask, was it the whole divine nature which constituted the divinity of Christ? If this question be answered in the affirmative, I desire to know where that divinity is which constitutes the other two persons in the Godhead. If the question be answered in the negative, and it be argued that the divinity which Christ possessed was an emanation from Jehovah, it is coming directly to what I contend for, viz. that he is a created being.

As we have seen from the prophecy of Daniel that Christ received his kingdom; so we are taught by St. Paul that he will deliver up his kingdom to the Father when he has accomplished the grand object of his reign, see 1 Cor. xv. 24-28:

> Then cometh the end, when he shall have delivered up the kingdom to God, even the Father: when he shall have put down all rule, and all authority, and power. For he must reign, till he hath put all enemies under his feet. The last enemy that shall be destroyed is death. For he hath put all things under his feet. But when he saith, all things are put under him, it is manifest that he is excepted which did put all things under him. And when all things shall be subdued unto him, then shall the Son also himself be subject unto him that put all things under him, that God may be all in all.

Enough, perhaps, is written on this part of our query to make the matter plain to the reader, although much more might be quoted from the scriptures in support of what we have argued.

I next inquire, has the Mediator power or ability to perform the great work of atonement, which is the reconciliation of the world to God? Those scriptures with their connections, which I have quoted to prove the Mediator's dependency, abundantly prove the sufficiency of his power to accomplish the work in which he is engaged. If all power in heaven and earth be committed to Christ, no doubt can be entertained of its sufficiency. If the whole system of law in moral nature be subservient to the designs of the Redeemer, and if he holds in his hands the power of moral government, it certainly must be at his option whether men shall be reconciled to God or not.

It may not be amiss to inquire in this place whether men, in their individual capacity, have the power of moral government. If they have, the great work of reconciliation might be performed by them, which would render the mission of Christ unnecessary. We ought not to suppose the Almighty ever purposed more than one way to produce the same event; if he has given ability to each individual to effect a complete reconciliation in himself, it is not consistent to believe that this work of reconciliation will be done by a Mediator; but if the work of reconciling all things to God is assigned to Christ, it is not reasonable to believe we have power to perform it ourselves. And I think it will not be deemed admissible that we have power to hinder this work of reconciliation, as that would, in effect, deny the truth of all power being given to Christ.

We ought to consider that Christ was by no means ignorant of man; that he needed none to testify of man, as he knew what was in man. He knew the moral distance which man had wandered from God, he knew all the expense of recovering him to holiness and happiness; and it appears rational that he knew whether he possessed ability to defray this expense or not; and if he knew he did not possess this ability, he would not have undertaken it. We ought not to suppose the Mediator would act as unwisely as a man who undertakes to build a large house without first counting the cost to know if he be able to finish a building so expensive; or as a king would do, who should make war on another king without first consulting whether he were able to contend with the double numbers which his adversary commanded.

St. Paul, writing to the Colossians, saith of Christ, he is the first born from the dead, that in all things he might have the pre-eminence; for it pleased the Father that in him all fullness should dwell; and that the Father had made peace, through the blood of his cross; and then informs them for what this peace was made; see chap. i. verse 20:

> By him to reconcile all things unto himself: by him, I say, whether they be things in earth, or things in heaven.

In Isaiah ix. 6, we have a beautiful prophetic testimony of the power and kingdom of the Savior:

> For unto us a child is born, unto us a son is given, and the government shall be upon his shoulder and his name shall be called Wonderful, Counsellor, the mighty God, the everlasting Father, the Prince of Peace.

And in the beginning of the next verse, the extent of his dominion is spoken of: "And of the increase of his government and peace there shall be no end."

There is a great number of like passages, which, in the course of this work, I shall have occasion to introduce; but enough is already quoted to show for what this power was given to Christ, and that it is sufficient to accomplish the end intended. Again, it may be reasonable to argue that if the Almighty committed power into the hands of Christ, for the performance of anything whatever, if there should be found, at last, a want of power for the work intended, it would prove a want of wisdom in the giver of such power. No one who professes to believe at all in Christ, will dispute his power for the performance of all his will.

But I wish to have the reader satisfied in respect to this power, and in what it consists, which, to make as clear as possible, I connect with our last particular in this general inquiry, which is atonement in its nature.

7. Atonement in Its Nature

I have already observed that atonement and reconciliation are the same. Reconciliation is a renewal of love, and love is the law of the spirit of life in Christ Jesus, of which St. Paul speaks in Romans viii. 2, by which he was made free from the law of sin. The soul, when governed by the law of sin which is in the members, of which St. Paul speaks in Romans vii. 23, is in a state of unreconciliation to the law of the spirit. And it is by the force and power of the law of love in Christ that the soul is delivered from the government of the law of sin; the process of this deliverance is the work of atonement, or reconciliation.

The reader will now see, with ease, that that power which causes us to hate sin and love holiness is the power of Christ, whereby atonement is made. All the law and the prophets rested on this spirit of love, by which alone they can be fulfilled.

Our Savior, in his official character, is always called by the names which are applicable to God manifest in the flesh. This circumstance will fully account for all the scriptures which my opponent would urge in support of Jesus' being essentially God.

Christ came not to destroy the law and the prophets, but to fulfill them; the law is as far fulfilled in the soul, as it is brought to love God in his adorable image, Jesus; and a complete fulfillment of the law and the prophets will effect love in every soul on whom the law, in a moral sense, is binding.

Let it be asked by what means are we brought to love God? Answer: "We love him because he first loved us." God's love to us is antecedent to our love to him, which refutes the notion of God's receiving the atonement; but the idea that the manifestation of God's love to us causes us to love him, and brings us to a renewal of love, is perfectly consonant to the necessity of atonement; it shows us what atonement is, and the power which the Mediator must have and exercise, in order to reconcile all things to God.

The method by which we are brought to love any object whatever is: by seeing or thinking we see some beauty in the object; and our love is always in proportion to the apparent good qualities of the object seen.

While our minds are darkened by the veil on the heart in reading of Moses, so that the beauties of the ministration of life are hidden from our eyes, and its excellent glories are out of our sight, it is impossible that we should love Christ or his word. Yet during this darkness, we must love something; therefore, as sin and the vanities of elementary life present the greatest beauty to our eyes, of any objects which we behold, our affections are placed on those corruptible things.

Now I call up the question again, has Jesus power to cause us to love holiness, and to hate sin? Answer: yes, if he has power to reveal the divine beauties of the word, to remove the letter and its administration which are death, to take the veil from the heart, and to cause us to see himself altogether lovely.

When a sinner views God as an enemy, and grumbles concerning his being hard and austere, when he feels an aversion to him and wishes to avoid his presence, it is certain the Son hath not revealed the Father to that soul. The ideas thus entertained of God are altogether wrong, and the mind that entertains them has no just conceptions of the Almighty. But blessed be the expressed image of the Invisible; he hath power to reveal the true character of the Father, to remove the veil from the heart, and to let the sunbeams of divine light gently into the understanding; then God appears altogether lovely, and the chiefest among ten thousand, while the soul in ecstasy embraces the brightness of his glory, crying, "My Lord, and my God." But the idea of the letter is so fixed in the minds of Christian people in general that the veil of the law is as fully on their hearts, as it was on the Pharisees of old, which caused them to be blind to their Messiah when he came.

Christians have for a long time believed that the temporal death of Christ made an atonement for sin, and that the literal blood of the man who was crucified has efficacy to cleanse from guilt; but surely this is carnality, and carnal mindedness, if we have any knowledge of the apostle's meaning where he says, "To be carnally minded is death." (Rom. viii. 6.) The letter killeth, but the spirit giveth life. The apostles were made able ministers of the new testament; not of the letter, but of the spirit. Christ saith, "Except ye eat my flesh, and drink my blood ye have no life in you." (John vi. 53.) Must we understand this in a literal sense? If we do, how shall we understand what he further says of this matter? (John vi. 63) —

The flesh profiteth nothing: the words that I speak unto you, they are spirit and they are life.

The apostasy of the Jews happened in consequence of the lips of the priests not preserving knowledge; they fell from the spirit of the law, were lost in the wilderness of the letter, and therefore were blinded. This was a figure of the more dreadful apostasy of Christians, as were various other circumstances recorded in the old testament. The Christian apostasy happened in the same way; and the church has been led into the wilderness of the letter by an hireling priesthood who knew nothing of the spirit of the law; who have preached, in the name of the Lord, the letter, which killeth, in room of the spirit, which giveth life.

I am sensible there are thousands who profess Christianity, who are blind enough to object and say, "Then the Gospel has nothing to do in the salvation of mankind." But suffer me to say the Gospel is nothing but the spirit of the law, which is the word, or *logos*, spoken in the law, brought forth from the shadows of the first dispensation. To believe in any other atonement than the putting off the old man, with his deeds, and the putting on of the new man, which after God is created in righteousness and true holiness, is carnal mindedness, and is death.

There is nothing in heaven above, nor in the earth beneath,

that can do away sin, but love; and we have reason to be thankful that love is stronger than death, that many waters cannot quench it, nor the floods drown it; that it hath power to remove the moral maladies of mankind, and to make us free from the law of sin and death, to reconcile us to God, and to wash us pure in the blood, or life, of the everlasting covenant. O love, thou great Physician of souls, what a work hast thou undertaken! All souls are thy patients; prosperous be thy labors, thou bruiser of the head of carnal mind.

In this view of the subject, we may see how the divine grace of reconciliation may be communicated to those who have never been privileged with the volume of divine revelation, and who have never heard the name of a Mediator proclaimed as the only way of life and salvation. I have no doubt but thousands whose education has taught them to look on the Christian religion as an imposture may possess a good degree of this love, which is the spirit of life in Christ Jesus; and though none can feel or experience this divine animation, only through the medium of the second Adam, we do not conceive that its agency is confined particularly to names, sects, denominations, people or kingdoms.

The word, which is nigh us, even in our hearts and mouths, is every where, operating, in some degree, in all hearts. The enmity which God put between the seed of the serpent and the seed of the woman is everywhere felt, and the two are struggling in every breast. When the creature-like nature or the carnal mind, which is enmity against God, leads the whole man captive, it is then that the soul is in a state of unreconciliation and death; but when the heavenly man, which, after God, is created in righteousness and true holiness, binds the strong man armed and whispers heavenly invitations to the soul, revealing himself in the understanding, the soul immediately ceases to confer with flesh and blood, beholds with inexpressible admiration the heavenly beauties of the new nature, is molded into its likeness and experimentally become a child of God; the way to the tree of life is opened and the soul enters by the anchor of hope within the veil, where the cherubims are disarmed of the flaming sword, and stand looking down on the mercy seat, where God communes with his people. Thus, by the spirit of the word, the soul is brought to a sweet communion with God; it feels its eternal sonship, and rejoices therein; with joy unspeakable and full of glory.

Perhaps the Christian reader will here pause and say: I can witness that what the author writes is true; but then, he does not tell of a regular law work, without which we can never be brought to taste those delicacies in the Gospel provisions. To this observation I reply: I believe there are as egregious errors crept into the Christian church, in this particular, as in anything relative to the Christian religion; and I further believe that among those who have really tasted that the Lord is gracious, there are such differences on the above point that, in many instances, they amount to a disfellowship, and tend greatly to destroy the blessed work begun in the heart. But those errors undoubtedly originate in some theories which are produced by the wisdom of the carnal mind, which is so opposed to the wisdom from above that it is always endeavoring to introduce something that may serve to raise animosities, and to sow discord among brethren.

Some, who by the force of a false education, have been led to believe that God is an enemy to the sinner have supposed they were every day exposed to the just vengeance of the Almighty, and have fancied that they could clearly see the justice of God in their eternal banishment from heaven and happiness; and they have been so wrecked on this wheel of torture as to be deprived of sleep and every kind of repose, for a tedious time, some longer and some shorter. Awful dreams, fraught with the most terrifying imaginations, have corroded the mind; and sometimes a burning lake of fire and brimstone has been painted so clearly, that, for several days together, the poor frightened soul would feel as if it were on the brink of a precipice expecting the next moment to be the fatal one.

In this awful situation, it pleases God to manifest himself; and in a moment, all those frightful imaginations are dispersed, and a universal calm takes possession of the whole region of the mind. The soul now rejoices as a captive set at liberty, or a pardoned criminal; and there is nothing to be heard from him but the praises of his Benefactor. In this hour of joy, should he hear ten thousand singing praises to his Redeemer, he would not wish to stop them to know whether they had all felt just as he had before he knew the truth. But in a short time, carnal mind, still alive in the members, begins to make its intrusions, and in a very deceitful way. It pretends to wish to help the soul along in religion, and says, there must be a close examination, it will not do to harbor errors, etc. But instead of setting the creature to examine himself, it sets him to examine his brother; his brother happens to be one who, in fact, loves Christ and his word, and to all appearance walks in the path of obedience. But his brother is one whose education was not quite so perverse as was his; his brother is one who was taught that God is an enemy to sin not to sinners; that he will chastise for iniquity, but that God is not so incensed as some imagine. This brother cannot tell all that his interrogator has experienced, and is therefore rejected for not telling a good law work.

It is now possible that the reader is more surprised than before, and will say the author does not talk like a Christian; and feeling some disagreeable emotion, he thinks he will read no further. But stop, dear sir; that determination may arise wholly from a want of divine charity. If you are, in reality, a Christian, and stand in the liberty wherewith Christ hath made you free, what you here read will do you no harm.

I am now about to examine your law work, as you call it, and shall argue that what you call law is only a creature of false education.

Before you found peace, you thought you could see the justice of God in your eternal exclusion from heaven and happiness. Now I ask, can you find that God ever gave a law to man which required endless misery in case of disobedience? Sure I am that the scriptures speak of none, neither do the dictates of good reason admit of its existence. Perhaps my opponent may say, we are not to use our reason in matters of religion. I answer, if we are not to understand the things of God by scripture and reason, we are at a loss to know how to come at them. I have before argued this point particularly in order to show that such a penalty does not exist in the law of God. Did you think an exclusion from heaven and happiness would be an exclusion from holiness and righteousness? Did you ever see the justice of God in your being sinful, unholy, and impure? You answer, no. Then you never saw the justice of God in your endless exclusion from heaven and happiness.

A false education has riveted the error in the minds of thousands, that God's law required endless misery to be inflicted on the sinner. How often do professed Christians address the Almighty, and say, "Hadst thou been just to have marked iniquity, we should, long since, have been in the grave with the dead, and in hell with the damned." This address amounts to nothing more, or less, than a complimental accusation against God of injustice! It surprises me to think now professed Christians will contend for the honor and glory of God in a way that renders his character infinitely inglorious and dishonorable.

Further, you believed (you say) before you were a believer in the truth that you stood in danger, every moment, of falling into endless misery. I would ask, if that were true, which you believed before you believed the truth? I further ask, are you now exposed to those dreadful torments? You will say, you hope for the better. And what is it that now preserves you from such danger? You confess it is your Savior. But was it not he who preserved you before your conversion? And are you more safe in his hands at one time than at another?

Some have gone so far in their law work as to say they saw

the justice of God so plainly, and it appeared so beautiful, that they were perfectly willing to be endlessly miserable, according to its requirements. Such Christians will not allow that a person can be savingly converted without being first willing to be endlessly miserable. This I must confess is a law work as unreconcilable to scripture and reason as it is corrosive to the mind. The amount of it is this: I see so much beauty and divine excellency in the justice of God that I am perfectly willing to exist, to all eternity, in rebellion against it! I wish to know what the soul has to be thankful for in the work of salvation? If it be brought to be willing to be endlessly miserable, it cannot be thankful for the gift of eternal life. Again, if a willingness to be damned is a good situation, we ought to continue in it; and then hell and endless woe would be as valuable a prize for which to run, in the Christian race, as heaven and immortality.

It is generally believed the Savior strives by his Spirit to bring the creature into a state of grace and salvation; and that the devil strives, with all his wily arts, to get the soul into hell and endless torments. Now, if these things be so, to which is the soul reconciled when it is willing to be endlessly miserable? That multitudes have been in great fear of being rejected by the Almighty at last, I have no doubt; for I confess those torments have been mine, in no small degree. But I contend it is impossible for any one to be willing to be endlessly miserable. Happiness always was, and always will be, the grand object of all rational beings; and to reverse this object would be to reverse man from a reasonable to an unreasonable creature.

The above notion of law work has been the awful means of driving multitudes of blinded mortals into as much despair as the mind is capable of. Honest-hearted persons who do not wish to be deceived, or to deceive others, knowing that they never felt willing to be damned, and being told they must be willing in order to be saved, have supposed that God had already reprobated their fearful souls to endless ruin! Others have been so deceived as to think they had better be willing to be damned than not to be saved; desiring salvation so much, they think they had better be willing to be shut out of heaven forever than to miss of salvation and have, either honestly or hypocritically, said they were willing to be damned; expecting great favors in consequence of the confession. The moment we have a just idea of the spirit of the law making an atonement for sin, all those absurdities and contradictions are removed, and their causes taken away.

I doubt not but God communicates his grace to persons laboring under every kind of deception; and in respect to that grace, no dispute arises among believers. Their disputes arise from notions which they entertained before they were enlightened, or from certain inventions of their own, afterwards, which do not arise from the spirit of truth.

The divine efficacy of this atoning grace may be communicated to the most vile and profligate person in the world, and stop him in his full career of wickedness; it can show the sinner, in a moment, the deformity of sin and the beauty of holiness. In other instances, the morally virtuous are led a long time in concern and great trouble about themselves before they find him of whom Moses and the prophets did write.

God is not confined to character, time or place, to work the work of atonement in the soul; he does all things well, and in the best time and way; and Christians do very wrong to contend about those differences which sin and deception caused in them before they knew Christ.

Two persons are discoursing about the agreeable flavor of the pineapple; one says to the other, it tastes very differently from what I expected it would before I tasted it; I thought it was a crabbed sour. Says the other, I am sure you never tasted of a pineapple; for before I tasted of one, I thought it was a disagreeable bitter. Thus they dispute, each in his turn arguing that the other had never tasted of the fruit, because they had different ideas about it before they actually had any knowledge of it.

Would you not, kind reader, advise those disputants to come to a solution of their question in a different way? Surely you would; and if they could agree about the real taste of the pineapple, you would advise them to let their former false notions alone.

Then, Christian reader, go and do likewise, in the religion of Jesus; and wherever you find a brother who has in reality tasted that the Lord is gracious, fellowship him as one initiated into the kingdom of God.

Atonement by Christ was never intended to perform impossibilities; therefore, it was never designed to make men agree and live in peace while they are destitute of love one to another; but it is calculated and designed to inspire the mind with that true love which will produce peace in Jesus. As atonement is a complete fulfillment of the law of the heavenly man, it causes its recipient to love God and his fellow creatures, in as great a degree as he partakes of its nature. Ask one brought out of darkness into the marvelous light of the Gospel, how God appears to him: and he will answer, more glorious than he can describe. Ask him how he feels towards his fellow men; and he will say, even of his enemies, he wishes them no worse than to enjoy the blessings of divine favor. In times of refreshing, how many thousands have been heard to speak of the goodness of the Lord, and of the infinite fullness of his grace; and with what love, affection, and fervency have they invited their fellow men to the rich provisions of the Gospel!

The earth, in time of drought, ceases to be fruitful; the streams and springs thereof are dried up; the fields put off their robes of green, and gardens afford no fragrant delights; but when the heavens give the wonted blessing in gentle showers, how suddenly is the face of nature changed! The purling rill murmurs through the mead, pastures and fields teem with vegetation, and gardens blush with enameled beauties.

So the soul, unwatered with the rain of righteousness, and

destitute of the waters of eternal life, is like a barren fig-tree that yields no wholesome fruit. But behold the transition; the moment atoning grace is effective in the mind, the parched ground becomes a pool, and the thirsty land, streams of water. The soul is like the earth that drinketh in the rain that cometh oft upon it, and bringeth forth herbs meet for them by whom they are dressed; and like a garden well watered and cultivated, yielding all manner of precious fruits.

Look on the trees after autumn has plucked their leaves, and winter frozen their trunks and limbs: Without faith in spring, their future life would be hopeless; but wait for the season of nature's appointment, when the increasing majesty of the sunbeams gently removes the chains of frost, and warm zephyrs are breathed on the surrounding snow, removing it from the land; the embryo blossom, nicely concealed in frost, now swells with genial heat; and the leaf, so nicely folded in winter's chest, now displays its matchless green, and the whole forest rejoices in expanded delights.

So if we look on man, in the sinful Adam, there is no appearance of heavenly life, or divine animation; the soul is bound in the fetters of sin, frozen with covetousness, and apparently dead in the winter of iniquity. But behold the Sun of righteousness arising with healing in his wings, removing sin by the power of grace, and killing moral death with divine life and animation, and causing the soul to rejoice in the kingdom of grace and glory. Then it may be rightly said (Song of Sol. ii. 11-12):

> The winter is past, the rains are over and gone, the flowers appear on the earth, and the time of singing is come.

How mysterious are the ways of God! What infinite depths of wisdom lie concealed from the sight of mortals! He who varies the seasons of the year, and diversifies nature through so great a number of changes without losing the smallest particle of matter, can carry his rational creatures through all the dispensations designed in infinite wisdom, without losing any, and consummate the whole in glory at last.

Suffer me, kind reader, in my faithfulness with the saints, to excite a close examination. It can be of no avail to believe we are partakers of atoning grace, unless that is really the case. I am of opinion that many may be deceived in these things; some may suppose they are experimentally acquainted with them, when in reality they have no other evidence of it than that some godly minister, as they suppose him to be, can fellowship them as Christians; while others do in reality feel this divine spirit of grace in its atoning operations, but dare not suffer themselves to believe it, because they have not obtained the approbation of some, in whom they have been taught to put confidence.

I would, therefore, note some faithful evidences in this case which will not deceive us; and in doing this, I shall keep the reader close to the spirit of the law, which is love to God and man. From these two points and their consequences, all the evidence which can be obtained must be deduced.

The question then is, do you love God? If you answer yes, I ask, why do you love him? —and why do you endeavor to serve him? If you answer: Because it is your duty and you fear his rod if you do not; I tell you, you are deceived; you have no real love to your Maker. Undoubtedly you would say (as many vain professors of Christianity have said), "If you were certain of salvation in the world to come, you would do all the mischief here you could." If the Gospel of Jesus Christ have any enemies in this wicked world, you are of that class. Your profession of Christianity, for forty or fifty years; your attention to church ordinances, and the mighty parade you have made in a round of (what you call) religious duties, have only served to paint you like a whited sepulcher. You lack the one thing needful, which is love.

You are ready to oppose all professors of Christianity who do not subscribe to your articles of faith. The weapons of your warfare are a tongue of slander, and a spirit of persecution; and you are daily raising false accusations against those who faithfully serve the Lord in spirit and in truth. The Pharisees of old made as great professions of religion as you do, and were as punctual to those customs; whereby they made void the law as you are to those whereby you make void the Gospel; and like you, they were zealous of defending their religion; and in their zeal they murdered the Lord of life and glory!

Perhaps you will say the author is hard in his reproofs. I reply, if you are not of the class of which we speak, you will not feel the rebuke; but if you are, you not only deserve it, but greatly need it. On the other hand, if you can truly say you love the Lord on account of the divine beauties and excellencies you behold in him; that he is in truth to you altogether lovely and the chiefest among ten thousand; that you delight in his service because it is your meat and drink to do his will; that your greatest enjoyment is obedience to his commands, which are joyous and not grievous, and in keeping of which there is great reward; let your denomination be what it may, let you live in what part of the world you will, you are a friend to the religion of Jesus, and you have sweet communion with him who sits at the right hand of God. Are you rich in the things of this world? —you view all your possessions at the will, and you wish to have them at the disposal, of the Master whom you serve. Are you adorned with titles of human honor? —how sweet is it to lay all these things at the feet of him whom you esteem infinitely honorable. Are you poor in the goods of fortune? —you possess the true riches. Are you a disconsolate widow? —behold God is your husband, and the father of your fatherless children.

Atoning grace produces all which the Bible means by conversion, or being born of the Spirit; it brings the mind from under the power and constitution of the earthly Adam, to live by faith on the Son of God, and to be ruled and governed, even in this life in a great measure, by the law of the spirit of life, in Christ Jesus. It opens eternal things to our view and contemplation; it brings heaven into the soul, and clothes the man in his right mind; it inspires the soul with divine meekness and boldness at the same time. It was this that enabled the apostles of our Lord to preach the Gospel, in defiance of the rage of their enemies, and gave them immortal consolations in their sufferings for the cause of truth. It causes the Christian to love all God's rational creatures, and to wish their saving knowledge of the truth; it produces good works in their purity, and all the morality worth the name is founded on it. Its divine power is stronger than any possible opposition, and the gates of hell cannot prevail against it; it opens a door of everlasting hope, and conducts the soul, by way of the cross, to immortality and eternal life. This dispensation of atonement is manifested through Christ, for the reconciliation of all things to God, in his glorious kingdom of holiness and happiness.

In this general view of atonement, we come to our last inquiry proposed in this treatise, namely, the consequences of atonement to mankind.

PART THREE: THE CONSEQUENCES OF ATONEMENT TO MANKIND

In this last inquiry, I must be a little more lengthy than in either of the former, but I hope not to be too tedious. What I shall contend for, as the consequences of atonement, is the universal holiness and happiness of mankind, in the final issue of the Redeemer's process. In doing this, I will—

First: Make a fair statement of the doctrine of universal salvation, as I understand it.

Secondly: Take notice of the most frequent objections stated against the doctrine by various denominations.

Lastly: Give my reasons for believing in my general proposition from scripture and reason.

8. Salvation Must Be Universal

Before I proceed to notice the direct proofs of the doctrine of the final holiness and happiness of all men, I shall notice some opposing doctrines and arguments and endeavor to obviate them by scripture and reason.

The first that I notice is found in a proposition frequently stated by modern divines thus: "God, in the great and infinite plan of moral government, consults the greatest possible good to the whole system; and in order for the greatest possible happiness to be produced, it was necessary that some of God's rational creatures should be eternally miserable: Agreeably to which, all men cannot be saved." This is the only ground on which an objection can be stated against universal holiness and happiness, while we admit the existence of an Infinite Supreme.

I cannot go into an examination of any authorities on which the above statement is supposed to stand; for I know of none. All I can do is to examine the statement itself. It is argued, agreeably to this proposition, that the infinite and inconceivable miseries of the wicked in the world to come will enhance the happiness of the glorified in heaven.

Against these statements I argue, if, in order for the greatest possible happiness to exist, the greatest possible misery must also exist, I wish to reverse the subject. Then the proposition would stand thus: In order for the greatest possible evil to exist, the greatest possible good must exist. Then if God, in his universal plan, has produced as much good as was possible, he has also produced as much evil as possible, which renders the statement that he consulted the greatest possible evil as just as that he consulted the greatest possible good. Of course, there is no more propriety in calling him good, than there is in calling him bad!

If it be said I carry this evil, or misery, too far, even beyond my opponent's meaning, I will endeavor to show him according to his own statement that I do not. He says every degree of misery in hell will produce many degrees of happiness in heaven; if so, if the wretched be not made as miserable as possible, the blessed cannot be made as happy as possible; if they are not made as happy as possible, they must experience some want; and, of course, some misery themselves. On the other hand, if the wretched be not as miserable as possible, they must have in possession some remaining convenience. Then, neither the greatest possible happiness, nor the greatest possible misery is produced.

Almighty God being put to the necessity of making some of his rational offspring eternally miserable, in order to make the rest forever happy, may be represented by a parent who has ten children; but only provisions enough to preserve the lives of five until he can get more. In this awful dilemma, he sits down to consult the greatest possible good; says to himself, if I divide my provisions equally among my children, all must surely starve to death; but by neglecting five, I can save the lives of the other five; which he finally concludes to do.

But I ask the rational, I petition the reasonable, I request the impartial to guess the feelings of a father on such an occasion! Before him are ten children, all in the image of himself; he sees his own eyes roll in their heads, hears his own voice on their tongues, while his own blood frolics through their veins; how could he make the division? how could he decide on one, for a victim? Would he not rather give his own flesh to be their meat, and his own blood to be their drink, and fervently pray for plenty!

But is the Almighty poor? Has he not enough and to spare? When the prodigal came home, did the father turn away his brother so that he might have a plenty for him? Is there not fullness enough in God to satisfy the wants of all his creatures? Why the necessity, then, of making some miserable eternally? My opponent will say the blessed are happified in consequence of the misery of the wretched. But what reason can be given for such an idea? How do we look on a person in this world who manifests joy and happiness in the misery of one of his fellow creatures? Do we say, he manifests a godlike disposition? Surely, no. From whence came charity? —from heaven. If souls in heaven possess it, they cannot be happy in consequence of the misery of any rational being.

Again, if a soul in heaven derives happiness from seeing, say, one-half or two-thirds of the human race in misery, would he not yet enjoy more, providing the whole, except himself, were in the same torment? If it be granted that he would, then in order for a soul to be made as happy as possible, the whole human race, except that one, must be endlessly as miserable as possible! If it be argued that it is not the number or multitudes of individuals who are made miserable that thus constitutes or enhances the happiness of the blessed, but that it is the nature, justice, and intenseness of this misery which is necessary for the above purpose, it makes it very plain that the eternal misery of one would produce as much good as of ten thousand, or more.

We have now got so far, even on our opponent's ground, as to see that there is no need of more than one soul's being endlessly miserable; and it still further appears to me that the misery of one may be dispensed with without departing from what my opponent has acknowledged; and that by letting each individual of the human race for a moment, or any limited time, experience the nature of the misery contended for; and then giving them a memory to retain it fresh in mind forever; this must of necessity produce the effect as well, and without the expense of a single soul. I do not think it would absolutely require omniscient wisdom to concert a better plan than the one I am opposing.

Suppose we alter the circumstance of the father and his ten children: suppose the father has provisions enough for the whole, and his object in the bestowing of it upon them is to cause the greatest possible happiness among his children. Which way would good sense and parental affection choose: either to feed five to the full and starve the rest to death that their dying groans might give the others a better appetite and their food a good relish; or to let them all be hungry enough to relish their food well, and all alike partake of it?

I will take notice of a certain passage of Scripture in this place, which some have endeavored to accommodate to the argument which I am disputing. See Rev. xiv. 10-11:

> The same shall drink of the wine of the wrath of God, which is poured out without mixture into the cup of his indignation; and he shall be tormented with fire and brimstone in the presence of the holy angels, and in the presence of the Lamb: and the smoke of their torment ascendeth up forever and ever: and they have no rest day nor night who worship the beast and his image, and whosoever receiveth the mark of his name.

It is not because I am afraid of wounding this beast, or of affronting its rider, that I do not enter into a particular explanation of the passage recited; but because it deserves the labor of more time than I have now to spare. However, the idea of my opponent is easily refuted; and this is as much as the reader ought to expect in this work. The common idea is, that the punishment here spoken of is altogether in eternity and not in this world of mortality; that it being in the presence of the holy angels, and in the presence of the Lamb, it indicates that it affords pleasure in those heavenly mansions where they dwell.

First, I request the reader to observe that the verbs "ascendeth," "have," "worship," and "receiveth" are all in the same tense, which at least favors the idea that the sulphurous smoke of this torment ascendeth up at the same time that the tormented worship the beast. If the apocalyptical beast be worshipped to an endless eternity, it follows that his worshippers will be tormented as long. Until it is proved that some will worship this beast in another world, or endlessly, it cannot be proved from this passage that any will be tormented in another world, or endlessly. It is said in the text that the worshippers of the beast have no rest day nor night. If it can be proved that day and night are reckoned in another world, or in eternity, my opponent has better ground for his argument than I think he has.

This beast, undoubtedly, is Antichrist; the worshippers of the beast are apostatized Christians of all denominations since the Christian apostasy. They have always been in wars and commotions, and have had no rest; and as for their being tormented in all their public worship with fire and brimstone, no argument is necessary to make it obvious.

Another objection, which has often been stated against the salvation of all men, stands in a pretended axiom, namely, "A God all mercy is a God unjust." The force of this pretended axiom as used against the salvation of all men is: if God should do justly by all men, he would be an unmerciful being; or, if he should show mercy to all men, he would be an unjust being. There is nothing self-evident in this axiom that I can see but its own want of propriety; it represents justice and mercy at an eternal variance. According to this axiom, and the argument deducible from it, justice may be compared to a monstrous wolf in pursuit of a number of lambs, and mercy to a shepherd who is obliged to give up a large number of them, to gorge his omnivorous appetite while he makes off with the rest.

I have already sufficiently refuted the idea of justice requiring the endless misery of the creature; and, until that notion can be supported by Scripture or reason, an objection against the salvation of all men cannot be stated from the nature of justice. I have also showed that in order for justice to require the endless misery of any moral being, it must of necessity require the endless continuance of sin, than which nothing is more absurd.

Again it is objected: as many are going out of this world daily in a state of sinfulness and unreconciliation to God, and there being no alteration in the soul for the better after it leaves this natural life, millions must be miserable as long as God exists.

The force of this objection stands on the supposition that there is no alteration for the better after death. Could this supposition be proved, I grant it would substantiate a formidable and (I think) an unanswerable objection against the final holiness and happiness of all men. I have often heard the objection made, but never heard an evidence brought from Scripture or reason to support the declaration. Divines being sensible of the want of Scripture to support this (their) supposition, have, very liberally, been at the expense of making some; and the notable passage which they have coined and brought into very frequent use is not to be found in the scriptures of the Old or New Testament; but is frequently to be heard from the pulpit, read in many of their writings, and recited by many of their adherents. It is as follows: "As the tree falls, so it lies; as death leaves us, so judgment will find us." I shall not contend about a different explanation of this addition to the Scriptures from the usual one; but will only say, if the thing which my opponents would prove by it be true, namely, that souls cannot be altered for the better after death, all our Christian people must remain eternally as unsanctified as they are in this world of infirmities.

Again, many contend that God deals with mankind as moral agents; that he sets life and death before us, and leaves us to make our own choice and to fare accordingly. That, as our eternal state depends on what use we make of our agency, millions will prove rebellious, and therefore miss of salvation. But I query, if one soul can obtain salvation on the principle of moral agency, why another cannot as well? If it be granted he can, I ask, again, why all men cannot as well as any? If it be still granted, I say, as I have before said, that which can be done may be done; therefore the objection fails. But the objector will say it renders universal salvation uncertain; I answer, no more than it renders universal damnation certain. All may be lost forever as well as one; therefore my opponent's hopes are subject to the same shipwreck to which he would expose mine. I would further inquire, if God deals with man upon a system of moral agency, is it God's revealed will that all men should be saved agreeably to their agency? If it be granted that it is, I further inquire whether God's will in the moral agency of man will be eternally frustrated? If not, no objection stands against Universalism; but the proposition on which my opponent endeavors to substantiate an objection favors the doctrine as far as it goes.

In my observations on the liberty of will, I have given some of my ideas concerning agency as it is generally understood; but moral agency may be very differently understood by different persons. If by moral agency ise meant an ability to love an object or objects which appear agreeable, I have no objections to make; but if it mean an ability to hate that which appears agreeable and to love that which appears disagreeable, I contend no such agency exists in any being within the compass of our knowledge. It is certainly reasonable to suppose that all the agency possessed by man was given him by his Maker; and that when God gave him this agency it was for a certain purpose, which purpose must finally be every way answered, providing God be infinitely wise. I cannot but think it incorrect to suppose that God ever gave any creature agency to perform what he never intended should be done. Then, if any soul be made endlessly miserable by its agency, it follows that God gave that soul this agency for that unhappy purpose; and if any be saved by their agency, God gave them their agency for that blessed end. If any wish to make a different use of agency, let them state fairly that God gave man an agency intending man's eternal salvation thereby; but man makes a different use of his agency from what God intended, whereby the gracious designs of Deity are forever lost!

If my opponent will not fix his agency on some of the above noted principles as it respects the issue of the argument, I am sure he can do nothing with it to any effect. If agency be stated on the principle of God's intending the creature's salvation by it, and it be granted that his will in the affair will be done, it is an acknowledgment of the doctrine for which I contend. But if it be stated that although God gave man his agency for the glorious purpose of his endless felicity, yet his purpose may fail. Could this statement be proved true, it would not only refute universal salvation, but everything else as being a divine system on which we may, with any confidence, depend.

9. The Most Frequent Objections Answered

One of the objections on which the enemies of universal holiness and happiness put much dependence, and which they frequently urge against the doctrine, is stated from the force of unlimited words, as they find a few of them in scripture applied to the misery of the wicked. The forces of this objection I remove by proving that unlimited words are applied to things and events which are not strictly eternal or endless; and surely the candid reader will acknowledge this way of reasoning is just, and by no means evasive. I shall not labor this point largely, for it has been done faithfully by an able author whose works are among us.

I will only introduce a few scriptures, and make some observations on them for the benefit of those of my readers who have not seen the masterly work referred to. See Gen. xvii. 7-8:

> And I will establish my covenant between me and thee, and thy see after thee in their generations, for an everlasting covenant; to be a God unto thee and thy seed after thee. And I will give unto thee, and to thy see after thee, the land wherein thou art a stranger, all the land of Canaan for an everlasting possession; and I will be their God.

Verse 13:
> He that is born in thy house, and he that is bought with thy money, must needs be circumcised; and my covenant shall be in your flesh for an everlasting covenant.

In the above passage the land of Canaan is called an everlasting possession. Will my opponent contend the word everlasting here means an endless duration? Will he contend that Abraham now possesses the land wherein he was then a stranger, or that his seed do, or will, possess that land as long as God exists? If not, then the objection is given up.

Again, the covenant of circumcision of the flesh is called an everlasting covenant. Will the objector contend that the covenant of circumcision in the flesh is now in force, and that it will remain in force as long as God exists? It is evident, from scripture, that these ordinances and this covenant are removed, and succeeded by a covenant which is called a better one; see Heb. viii. 6-8:

> But now hath he obtained a more excellent ministry, by how much also he is the Mediator of a better covenant which was established upon better promises. For if that first covenant had been faultless, then should no place have been sought for the second. For finding fault with them, he saith, behold, the days come, saith the Lord, when I will make a new covenant with the house of Israel and with the house of Judah.

In chap. ix. 10, the apostle argues that the ordinances of the first covenant were imposed on the people until the time of reformation. In Gen. xlviii. 3-4:

> And Jacob said unto Joseph, God Almighty appeared unto me at Luz in the land of Canaan, and blessed me; and said unto me, behold, I will make thee fruitful, and multiply thee, and I will make of thee a multitude of people; and will give this land to thy seed after thee for an everlasting possession.

And he further said, in the blessing of Joseph (Gen. xlviii. 26):

> The blessings of thy father have prevailed above the blessings of my progenitors unto the utmost bounds of the everlasting hills.

Exod. xl. 15:

> And thou shalt anoint them (Aaron's sons) as thou didst anoint their father, that they may minister unto me in the priest's office; for their anointing shall surely be an everlasting priesthood throughout their generations.

Lev. xvi. 34:

> And this shall be an everlasting statute unto you, to make an atonement for the children of Israel for all their sins once a year. And he did as the Lord commanded Moses.

The reader may learn the abolishment of the priesthood, from Heb. vii. 11-12:

If, therefore, perfection were by the Levitical priesthood (for under it the people received the law), what further need was there that another priest should rise after the order of Melchisedec, and not be called after the order of Aaron? For the priesthood being changed, there is made of necessity a change also of the law.

Jonah ii. 6:

I went down to the bottoms of the mountains; the earth with her bars was about me forever: yet hast thou brought up my life from corruption, O Lord my God.

Many more passages might be quoted to clear this point of argument, if more were necessary; but depending some, as I ought to, on the candor of my reader, I forbear to be tedious.

In the next place, I will take notice of a number of scriptures in connection, all of which have been erroneously applied to the future and endless misery of mankind. See Mal. iv. 1:

For behold, the day cometh that shall burn as an oven, and all the proud, yea, and all that do wickedly, shall be stubble, and the day that cometh shall burn them up, saith the Lord of hosts, that it shall leave them neither root nor branch.

Matt. iii. 10:

And now also the axe is laid unto the root of the trees: therefore every tree which bringeth not forth good fruit is hewn down, and cast into the fire.

Verse 12:

Whose fan is in his hand, and he will thoroughly purge his floor, and gather his wheat into the garner, but the chaff we will burn with unquenchable fire.

Chap. v. 29-30:

And if thy right eye offend thee, pluck it out and cast it from thee; for it is profitable for thee that one of thy members should perish, and not that thy whole body should be cast into hell.

Chap. vii. 13-14:

Enter in at the strait gate: for wide is the gate, and broad is the way that leadeth to destruction, and many there be which go in thereat: because strait is the gate, and narrow is the way which leadeth unto life, and few there be that find it.

Chap. xiii. 30:

Let both grow together until the time of harvest; and in time of harvest I will say unto the reapers, gather ye together, first the tares, and bind them in bundles to burn them; but gather the wheat into my barn.

The whole of Chap. xxv., which is too lengthy to be written at large. The last paragraph of Luke xvi. And 2 Thess. i. 7-9:

And to you who are troubled, rest with us, when the Lord Jesus shall be revealed from heaven with his mighty angels, in flaming fire, taking vengeance on them that know not God, and that obey not the gospel of our Lord Jesus Christ; who shall be punished with everlasting destruction from the presence of the Lord and from the glory of his power.

There are a number more scriptures of the like nature of the above quoted, to which I should be glad to attend, were it not for swelling this work too large. I will, however, after I have answered these in their order, take into consideration some others of a different kind. Those which I have quoted respect that dispensation which is represented by fire. Therefore in all the passages recited, it is evident the same fire is intended. "For behold, the day cometh that shall burn as an oven." (Mal. iv. 1.) In this same chapter, this day is called the great and dreadful day of the Lord, who promised to send Elijah the prophet before that day come, whose business should be to turn the hearts of the fathers to the children, and the hearts of the children to their fathers, lest the Lord should smite the earth with a curse.

I inquire, first, concerning the coming of this prophet, in order to fix on a time for the commencement of this day of the Lord. That Elijah and Elias are the same, in scripture, no doubt will be entertained. Then turn to Matt. xvii. 12-13:

But I say unto you that Elias is come already, and they knew him not, but have done unto him whatsoever they listed; likewise shall also the Son of Man suffer of them. Then the disciples understood that he spake unto them of John the Baptist.

By this scripture it appears that the promise of the coming of Elijah the prophet was fulfilled by the coming of John the Baptist, who came in the spirit and power of Elias.

This evidently justifies the belief that the great and dreadful day of the Lord, to which the prophet alluded, would soon follow the coming of John the Baptist. Agreeably to this fact we find all which is written in the New Testament on the same subject. By careful attention to the instructions of Jesus, we shall find that all those scriptures were fulfilled in the generation in which he lived in the flesh. Matt. xvi. 27-28:

> For the son of man shall come in the glory of his Father, with his angels; and then he shall reward every man according to his works. Verily I say unto you there be some standing here which shall not taste of death till they see the Son of man coming in his kingdom.

Respecting this passage we desire the reader to notice the following particulars: First: Jesus speaks of his coming in glory of his Father with his angels at some time in the future. Second: He is careful to state, as the principal fact communicated in this passage, that when he should so come as he had described, he would render unto every man according to his works. Here we have a statement of a certain time, which would be a Day of Judgment in which every man would receive according to his works. This Day of Judgment is unquestionably the Day of Judgment elsewhere spoken of in the teaching of Jesus and his apostles. Third: Jesus is careful to fix the time of this judgment, not to a day nor to an hour, but emphatically does he limit it within the lifetime of some of those to whom he spake.

Of this day of trial we read again in Mark viii. 38; ix. 1:

> Whosoever, therefore, shall be ashamed of me and of my words in this adulterous and sinful generation, of him also shall the Son of man be ashamed, when he cometh in the glory

of his Father, with the holy angels. And he said unto them, Verily I say unto you, that there be some standing here, which shall not taste of death, till they have seen the kingdom of God come with power.

Here I again request the reader to observe that the same particulars, which were notices in respect to the former passage, are found to be contained in this: Luke ix. 26-27:

> For whosoever shall be ashamed of me, and of my words, of him shall the Son of man be ashamed, when he shall come in his own glory, and in his Father's , and of the holy angels. But I tell you of a truth, there be some standing here, which shall not taste of death, till they see the kingdom of God.

What I desired the reader to observe in the former passages, he will also notice in this.

Should the objector contend that the coming of Christ in his glory, with his angels, to reward men according to their works, as set forth in the preceding passages, cannot be the same with his coming at the end of the world, of which mention is made in Matt. xxiv., I reply by informing him that if he will so far divest himself of the prejudices of his education as to give this subject a candid investigation, I soberly believe that he will arrive at an entire conviction that the coming of Jesus at the end of the world, of which he speaks in Matt. xxiv., did correspond with his coming as expressed in those passages above quoted, and did take place in the generation in which he lived on the earth.

But I deem it expedient to show that not only the coming of Christ, as pointed out in these scriptures, took place in that generation, but also that the "great and dreadful day of the Lord" which was to burn as an oven, by which all the proud, yea, and all who did wickedly became stubble, also came in that generation. And that this day was the end of the world, of which Jesus spake Matt. xxiv. Furthermore, that we have the following account of the same end of the world in Matt. xiii. 40-42:

> As therefore the tares are gathered and burned in the fire; so shall it be in the end of this world. The son of man shall send

forth his angels, and they shall gather out of his kingdom all things that offend, and them which do iniquity, and shall cast them into a furnace of fire: there shall be wailing and gnashing of teeth.

And moreover that within the same specified period all the dreadful judgments which he denounced were fulfilled.

Keep in mind how carefully Jesus stated, in the passages above quoted, that some of them to whom he spake should live to see the time of his coming with his angels to render unto every man according to his works, and pass to an examination of other passages. Matt. x. 23:

> But when they persecute you in this city, flee ye into another; for verily, I say unto you, ye shall not have gone over the cities of Israel till the son of man be come.

Here take particular notice of the following circumstances. First: The divine master is giving his disciples special directions in relation to the prudence which they would need to exercise while accomplishing the labors to which he had appointed them. Second: For a season this caution would be necessary on account of the persecutions to which the disciples would be exposed; but they were encouraged to expect a change for their benefit, when Jesus should come, according to his promises. In support of this fact see Luke xxi. 28-32:

> And when these things begin to take place, then look up, and lift up your heads; for your redemption draweth nigh. And he spake to them a parable; Behold the fig tree and all the trees: when they new shoot forth, ye see and know of your own selves that summer is now nigh at hand. So likewise ye when ye see these things come to pass, know ye that the kingdom of God is nigh at hand. Verily I say unto you, this generation shall not pass away till all be fulfilled.

Third: The divine master certifies his disciples that they should not have past over the cities of Israel till he should come. This was fixing his coming within the time of their ministry. Look next at the war which Jesus denounced on his enemies, the Jews, as recorded in Matt. xxiii. After a lengthy and a most severe annunciation of war on the scribes and Pharisees, Jesus brings this last address to them to a close, as follows (Matt. xxiii. 32-39):

> Fill ye up then the measure of your fathers. Ye serpents, ye generation of vipers! how can ye escape the damnation of hell? Wherefore, behold, I send unto you prophets, and wise men, and scribes; and some of them ye shall kill and crucify; and some of them shall ye scourge in your synagogues, and persecute them from city to city; that upon you may come all the righteous blood, shed upon the earth, from the blood of righteous Abel unto the blood of Zacharias, son of Barathias, whom ye slew between the temple and the altar. Verily I say unto you, all these things shall come upon this generation. O Jerusalem, Jerusalem, thou that killest the prophets, and stonest them which are sent unto thee, how often would I have gathered thy children together even as a hen gathereth her chickens under her wings and ye would not! Behold your house is left unto you desolate. For I say unto you, ye shall not see me henceforth, till ye shall say blessed is he that cometh in the name of the Lord.

Let the reader be careful to observe that according to this passage the damnation of hell and all the war here denounced were to come on that people in that generation.

After Jesus had finished this tremendous address which he delivered to the Jews in their temple, the last time he spake there, we are informed Matt. xxiv. 1-2 that:

> Jesus went out and departed from the temple: and his disciples came to him, for to show him the buildings of the temple. And Jesus said unto them, see ye not all these things, Verily I say unto you there shall not be left here one stone upon another, that shall not be thrown down.

This assurance which Jesus gave to his disciples, that of that beautiful temple not one stone should be left upon another that should not be thrown down, was in reference to what they had just heard him state in the temple concerning its desolation (chap. xxiv. 3):

And as he sat upon the mount of Olives, the disciples came unto him privately, saying tell us, when shall these things be? and what shall be the sign of thy coming, and of the end of the world?

Here be careful to observe that the *things* of which the disciples spake when they asked, "when shall these things be?" were those things of which Jesus had just spoken in the temple. In his reply to the questions which his disciples asked him, Jesus is careful to give clear and definite answers. He first warned them against being deceived by the many who would come in his name, and deceive many. Chap. xxiv, 6, etc.:

And ye shall hear of wars, and rumors of wars: See that ye be not troubled; for all these things must come to pass, but the end is not yet.

It seems proper in this place to ask what Jesus meant by the end, which he said "is not yet." Surely the true answer to this question is found in the questions which his disciples asked him, to which he was then answering. The questions which they asked him were the following. "When shall these things be? and what shall be the sign of thy coming, and of the end of the world?" It was the end of world which Jesus said in verse 6, "is not yet." Jesus goes on to give further particulars concerning events which would come to pass before the end of the world; and speaks of the rising of nation against nation, and kingdom against kingdom, and of earthquakes in diverse places. Also of the persecutions which the disciples should suffer; but tells them, verse 13, "He that shall endure unto the end, the same shall be saved"; and then adds (verse 14):

and this gospel of the kingdom shall be preached in all the world, for a witness unto all nations; and then shall the end come.

That is the end of the world of which the disciples asked their Master. We have often heard preachers attempt to describe the end of the world, arid its attendant circumstances, with zeal and vehemency, in which they would speak of the dissolution of the earth, the dissolving of the sun, of the moon, and the stars; of the resurrection of all the dead, and of their coming to judgment; of the august appearance of Jesus surrounded with a multitude of the heavenly hosts, who are to wait on him while he sits in judgment to decide the destinies of the whole human family forever and ever. This scene they lay altogether in what they call eternity.

Such being the views entertained by the objector, he feels confident that the coming of Christ at the end of the world could not have taken place in that generation. But I would respectfully invite him to attend to certain descriptions which Jesus gave of the end of the world, and of certain circumstances which would attend it. He goes on thus (Matt. xxiv. 15-21):

> When ye, therefore, shall see the abomination of desolation, spoken of by Daniel the prophet, stand in the holy place (whoso readeth let him understand) then let them which be in Judea flee into the mountains: let him which is on the housetop not come down to take any thing out of his house: neither let him which is in the field return to take any thing out of his house. And woe unto them that are with child, and to them that give suck in those days! But pray ye that your flight be not in the winter, neither on the sabbath day! For there shall be great tribulation, such as was not since the beginning of the world to this time, no, nor ever shall be.

Concerning this description, let us carefully notice several particulars:— First: Jesus gives his disciples to understand that at this end of the world they would see the abomination of desolation, spoken of by Daniel the prophet, stand in the holy place. If we turn to Daniel we may be satisfied whether the prophet spake of what would take place in this state of man's existence, or in what, is commonly called eternity. See Dan. ix, 26:

> And after threescore and two weeks shall Messiah be cut off, but not for himself: and the people of the prince that shall come shall destroy the city, and the sanctuary; and the end thereof shall be with a flood, and unto the end of the war desolations are determined.

Chap. xii. 11:
> And from the time that the daily sacrifice shall be taken away, and the abomination that maketh desolate, set up, there shall be a thousand two hundred and ninety days.

Such descriptions may well apply to the calamitous wars which wasted the Jews, overthrew their city, and planted the Roman standard in the temple of God, even in the holy place. But we hardly think our objector will be disposed to apply such representations to events which are to take place in a future state.

Secondly: At the end of the world of which Jesus spake to his disciples, and when they should see the abomination of desolation, spoken of by Daniel the prophet, stand in the holy place, he told them who were in Judea to flee into the mountains. This advice was undoubtedly very judicious, if the occasion of their flight was the dire calamity of war; but if the occasion were the annihilation of the material universe, the resurrection of all the dead, and the assembling of the whole human race to the solemnities of what is called the eternal judgment, it is difficult to understand how security could be obtained by fleeing into the mountains.

Thirdly: Jesus signified to his disciples that the end of the world would be a season of difficulty which would be augmented if it should happen in the winter or on the sabbath. These suggestions were very correct if they referred to temporal inconveniences; but it would be difficult to understand how to apply them to scenes in the invisible world.

Fourth: Jesus gave his disciples to understand that the troubles which would come on the people at the end of the world would fall with peculiar inconvenience on such as should at that time be with child or should give suck to their infants. We have little doubt that our objector will see that these circumstances may apply much better to temporal inconveniences endured by females during the terrible storm of war and the conquest of their city, than to any event in eternity of which we read in the scriptures.

That all these events, including the end of the world, the coming of the Son of man with his angels, etc., took place in the generation in which the Savior lived on earth, we are fully certified by his own words which follow (Matt. xxiv. 30-35):

> And then shall appear the sign of the Son of man in heaven: and then shall all the tribes of the earth mourn, and they shall see the Son of man coming in the clouds of heaven with power and great glory. And he shall send his angels with a great sound of a trumpet, and they shall gather together his elect from the four winds, and from one end of heaven to the other. Now learn a parable of the fig-tree; when his branch is yet tender, and putteth forth leaves, ye know that summer is nigh: so likewise ye when ye, shall see all these things, know that it is near, even at the doors. Verily I say unto you, this generation shall not pass till all these things be fulfilled. Heaven and earth shall pass away, but my word shall not pass away.

It seems worthy of special notice that in every instance in which Jesus spake of his coming to judge men, and to reward them according to their works, he expresses himself with peculiar emphasis in limiting the time to the generation in which he lived. Matt xvi. 28: "Verily I say unto you," etc. Mark ix. 1: "Verily I say unto you," etc. Luke ix, 27: "But I tell you of a truth," etc. Matt. x. 23: "For Verily I say unto you," etc. Luke xxi. 32: "Verily I say unto you," etc. Matt, xxiii. 36: "Verily I say unto you," etc. Matt. xxiv. 34: "Verily I say unto you, this generation shall not pass till all these things be fulfilled." I think I am safe in saying that on no other one subject did Jesus express himself with more cautious emphasis. Have we not then great reason to marvel that so many of those who are professed disciples of Jesus, and who profess to preach his word to the people, should ever have so misconstrued his testimony as to represent his coming with his angels to reward men is to take place in some time which is now future, and in another state of man's existence?

After Jesus had certified his disciples that all those events of which he spoke would take place in that generation, he proceeded to say to them (Matt. xxiv. 36):

> But of that day and hour knoweth no man, no, not the angels of heaven, but my Father only.

And this circumstance he improved to show the necessity of due watchfulness in his disciples, that they might avail themselves of the benefits of his instructions, and make their escape from those calamities which were fast approaching. In the latter part of this chapter he strictly warned them to be on their guard, and duly apprised them of the danger which awaited them should they so far relax in their watchings as to become contentious and to eat and drink with the drunken, thinking that their Lord delayed his coming, assuring them that should any be found of this description, the Lord of such a servant would come in a day when he looked not for him, and in an hour that he would not be aware of, and would cut him asunder, and appoint him his portion with the hypocrites; where there should be weeping and gnashing of teeth. As Jesus had, in hearing of his disciples, just delivered his last address to the scribes and Pharisees in the temple, and as he had denounced on them the most tremendous judgments, calling them hypocrites, which epithet he often repeated in that discourse; he now informs his disciples, being alone with them, that if any of them should so far apostatize as to conform their lives to the sinfulness of that wicked and perverse generation, they would of course fall into the same condemnation, which he had just denounced on those whom he called hypocrites, and would be subjected to the same awful calamities.

This Jesus represented by the two following parables: that of the ten virgins, and that of the talents. Let it be duly observed, that the parables recorded in the twenty-fifth chapter of Matthew were all designed to represent the things which are stated in the twenty-fourth chapter. —The division of chapters very frequently disjoins a well-connected discourse in such an abrupt manner as to entirely obscure the sense; unless the reader is careful, by disregarding this arbitrary division, to preserve the connection by reading directly on. When Jesus had stated to his disciples the danger they would expose themselves to, by getting off their guard, as has been noticed, he added (Matt. xxv. 1):

> Then shall the kingdom of heaven be likened unto ten virgins, which took their lamps, and went forth to meet the bridegroom.

In order to preserve the connection in this reading, we ask the question when did Jesus mean that the kingdom of heaven should be likened unto ten virgins? He says, "Then...." And this word then begins the twenty-fifth chapter.

Suppose a person sits down to read a chapter in the New Testament; and without paying any attention to any thing that is said in the twenty-fourth chapter, begins the twenty-fifth and reads it through, how could he understand what the three parables, which occupy the whole chapter, were designed to represent? He would know nothing about the subjects for the illustration of which the parables were spoken. He would have no idea concerning the time to which the first word in the chapter referred. But by looking back we find that the word "then" refers to the time just mentioned, thus: "The Lord of that servant shall come in a day when he looketh not for him" (Matt. xxiv. 50), etc. But here we are not told when that day would be. We must then look back still farther. See chap. xxiv. 44:

> Therefore be ye also ready; for in such an hour as ye think not, the Son of man cometh.

This does not fix the time. The fact is, neither that day nor that hour are designated in the whole discourse. See chap. xxiv. 36 etc.:

> But of that day and hour knoweth no man, no, not the angels of heaven, but my Father only.

And: "But of that day and hour." What day and hour? That day must refer to some time of which notice had been taken before. Look back then to the two preceding verses (chap. xxiv. 34-35):

> Verily I say unto you, this generation shall not pass till all these

things be fulfilled. Heaven and earth shall pass away, but my word shall not pass away.

By this method, I arrive at the fact that Jesus spake of no time, of no day nor hour in all that follows these last words quoted, that was not limited to that generation.

By being thus cautious we find our subject all laid open as clearly as the sun shines. The parable of the ten virgins, and also that of the talents, were designed to set forth what the divine teacher had just stated respecting how it would fare with those who were his professed disciples, at the time when Jerusalem should be destroyed by the Romans. With this fact in the mind, read the last paragraph of the twenty-fourth chapter, and the two first of the twenty-fifth, in connection with one another.

The nuptial ceremonies among the Jews were familiar to the disciples of Jesus; and so was the custom of letting money at interest. These two customs he used to impress on their minds the necessity of being on their guard that they might be prepared for the occasion of their Lord's coming; and also duly to improve the gifts which he had bestowed on them, that at his coming they might be able to present him with suitable improvements.

If I duly consider what I have here collected from the directions which Jesus gave to his disciples, and remember that he told them, as has been noticed, Matt. x. 23:

But when they persecute you in this city, flee ye into another; for verily I say unto you, ye shall not have gone over the cities of Israel till the son of man be come,

I must not only feel a full conviction that the common use which has been made of these parables of the virgins and the talents is altogether foreign from the Savior's meaning, but I must also feel no small surprise at such an egregious error.

We come now to notice the parable of the sheep and goats. Immediately following the conclusion of the parable of the talents, Jesus says (Matt. xxv. 32 etc.):

> When the Son of man shall come in his glory, and all the holy angels with him, then shall he sit upon the throne of his glory, etc.

Then follows an account of the judgment. Here let it be observed that the Savior, having instructed his disciples respecting what he should require of them, and how they would be rewarded for their faithfulness, or punished for their delinquency, proceeds to represent the great distinction which would, at the same time, be made between these who should treat them kindly, and those who should neglect so to do.

Let us be duly cautious concerning the time of the coming of the Son of man, in his glory, and with his angels. In this parable he gives no intimation when this coming would take place, or when it ought to be expected. The reason why he did not mention the time is the same for which he did not point out the day nor hour of his coming in the preceding context. The reason, in all these cases, why he did not mention the particular time was because he had explicitly stated that his coming with his angels would certainly be in that generation; but that of the day and the hour none but his Father in heaven knew. The reader is here requested to keep in mind all those passages which have been quoted, which speak of the coming of Jesus with his angels, etc., and to remember that they all expressly state that his coming would be during that generation.

It is contended by some that if the former parables in this twenty-fifth chapter of Matthew refer to the time of that generation, this parable of the sheep and goats refers to a general judgment in the future state after the material universe is dissolved, and all mankind are raised into an immortal state. But surely there is not the least authority for this conclusion. There is nothing hinted respecting the dissolution of the material universe; not a word said about the resurrection of the dead.

In this parable of the sheep and goats we have the following particulars represented. First: The King, who sits as judge. Second: Two classes, one on the right hand of the King, the other on his left. These two classes are separated one from the other, and they are differently treated on account of the difference there was in their conduct to another, or a third class. This third class were the disciples of Jesus, to whom he spake the parable; and whom he calls his brethren. By this parable Jesus seemed to say to his disciples:— Brethren, as you travel from city to city to publish the gospel of my kingdom, in my name, I shall regard every act of kindness and hospitality done to you, by people where you labor, as done to myself; and also all the cold hearted neglect which shall mark the conduct of people towards you, I shall consider as done to me. In agreement with this, see Matt. x. 40-42:

> He that receiveth you, receiveth me; and he that receiveth me, receiveth him that sent me. He that receiveth a prophet, in the name of a prophet, shall receive a prophet's reward: and he that receiveth a righteous man, in the name of a righteous man shall receive a righteous man's reward. And whosoever shall give to drink unto one of these little ones a cup of cold water only in the name of a disciple, verily I say unto you, he shall in no wise lose his reward.

Verses 12-15:

> And when ye come into an house, salute it. And if the house be worthy, let your peace come upon it: but if it be not worthy, let you peace return to you. And whosoever shall not receive you, nor hear your words, when ye depart out of that house or city shake off the dust of your feet. Verily I say unto you, it shall be more tolerable for the land of Sodom and Gomorrah in the day of judgment, than for that city.

After having satisfied our minds respecting the time of the coming of the Son of man to judge and reward men according to their works, and being assured that that event took place when Jerusalem was destroyed, and the Jews dispersed, it remains an easy task to settle the question respecting the meaning and fulfillment of all the passages in the New Testament which speak of that judgment, and the awful calamities which fell on that people.

But we must always keep in mind the fact that all those scriptures were fulfilled in that generation in which Jesus and his disciples lived.

Let us notice the following passages in connection, as they evidently belong to the same subject. Matt. iii. 10:

> And now also the axe is laid at the root of the trees: therefore, every tree that bringeth not forth good fruit is hewn down and cast into the fire.

Verse 12:

> Whose fan is in his hand, and he will thoroughly purge his floor, and gather his wheat into his garner, but the chaff he will burn with unquenchable fire.

Chap. v. 29-30:

> And if thy right eye offend thee, pluck it out and cast it from thee; for it is profitable for thee, that one of thy members should perish, and not that thy whole body should be cast into hell.

Chap. xiii. 30:

> Let both grow together until the harvest; and in the time of harvest I will say to the reapers gather ye together first the tares, and bind them in bundles to burn them; but gather the wheat into my barn.

2 Thess. i. 7-10:

> And to you who are troubled rest with us, when the Lord Jesus shall be revealed from heaven with his mighty angels, in flaming fire, taking vengeance on them that know not God and that obey not the Gospel of our Lord Jesus Christ; who shall be punished with everlasting destruction from the presence of the Lord, and from the glory of his power; when he shall come to be glorified in his saints, and to be admired; in all them that believe (because our testimony among you was believed,) in that day.

That these and some other passages all refer to the same time and events as are pointed out in Matt. 24 and 25, which we have noticed, there will be no doubts with any. Those who are opposed to my views apply them all to a future state of punishment. It is therefore unnecessary to explain them separately. It is evident that the burning of the chaff, as expressed Matt. iii. 12, and the being cast into hell, expressed chap. v. 30, and the burning of the tares, of which we read chap, xiii, 30; and the being punished with everlasting destruction, recorded 2 Thess. i. 9, all mean the same thing. It is also evident that the end of the world, of which we read in Matt. xx. 24, which Jesus carefully and emphatically confined to the generation in which he lived, as we have fully seen, and the end of the world of which he spake in his exposition of the parable of the tares; see Matt. xiii. 40-42:

> Therefore tares are gathered and burned in the fire; so shall it be in the end of this world. The Son of man shall send forth his angels, and they shall gather out of his kingdom all things that offend and them that do iniquity, and shall cast them into a furnace, of fire; there shall be wailing and gnashing of teeth.

The reader may be at a loss to know why Jesus should call the time of his coming to destroy Jerusalem, the end of the world. We say then it was because it was the end of the Jewish state and polity; and it was the commencement of a new era and a new order of things. The word rendered "world" should have been rendered "age." See Heb. ix. 26:

> But now once, in the end of the world, hath he appeared to put away sin by the sacrifice of himself.

Also 1 Cor. x. 11:

> Now all these things happened unto them for ensamples; and they are written for our admonition, upon whom the ends of the world are come.

Such an end of the world as our preachers are talking of, and which they use to frighten people, is now here spoken of in the scriptures.

That it was natural for Jesus to represent the sore afflictions which he saw coming on the house of Israel, by everlasting fire, by unquenchable fire, and by hell fire, we learn by referring to the language used to represent the same things in the Old Testament. See Ezekiel xxii. 18-22:

> Son of man, the house of Israel is to me become dross; all they are brass, and tin, and iron, and lead in the midst of the furnace; they are even the dross of silver. Therefore saith the Lord God, because ye are all become dross, behold, therefore, I will gather you into the midst of Jerusalem. As they gather silver, and brass, and iron, and lead and tin into the midst of the furnace, to blow the fire upon it, to melt it; so will 1 gather you in my anger and in my fury, and I will leave you there, and melt you. Yea, I will gather you, and blow upon you in the fire of my wrath, and ye shall be melted in the midst thereof. As silver is melted in the midst of the furnace, so shall ye be melted in the midst thereof; and ye shall know that I the Lord have poured out my fury upon you.

Chap. xxi. 30-32:

> Shall I cause it to return into his sheath? I will judge thee in the place where thou wast created, in the land of thy nativity. And I will pour out mine indignation upon thee; I will blow against thee in the fire of my wrath, and deliver thee into the hand of brutish men and skilful to destroy. Thou shalt be for fuel to the fire; thy blood shall be in the midst of the land;. thou shalt be no more remembered; for I the Lord have spoken it.

Isaiah ix. 19:

> Through the wrath of the Lord of hosts is the land darkened, and the people shall be as the fuel of the fire; no man shall spare his brother.

In bringing the subject of those scriptures, which speak of consuming the wicked by fire, to a close, I judge it proper to notice that not only are those awful judgments which we have noticed represented by fire; but fire also is used to represent the purifying power of divine truth. And it is evident that both these uses of fire are embraced in those scriptures which we have passed in review. The following passage seems to present both these ideas: Mal. iii. 1-3:

> Behold, I will send my messenger, and he shall prepare the way before me, and the Lord, whom ye seek, shall suddenly come to his temple, even the messenger of the covenant whom ye delight in: behold, he shall come, saith the Lord of hosts. But who may abide the day of his coming? And who shall stand when he appeareth? for he is like a refiner's fire, and like fuller's soap. And he shall sit as a refiner and purifier of silver; and he shall purify the sons of Levi, and purge them as gold and silver, that they may offer unto the Lord an offering in righteousness.

The same things appear in the passage in Matthew which has been noticed, chap. iii. 10-12:

> And now also the axe is laid unto the root of the trees; Therefore every tree which bringeth not forth good fruit is hewn down and cast into the fire. I indeed baptize you with water unto repentance; but he that cometh after me is mightier than I, whose shoes I am not worthy to bear; he shall baptize you with the Holy Ghost and with fire; whose fan is in his hand, and he will thoroughly purge his floor, and gather his wheat into his garner; but he will burn up the chaff with unquenchable fire.

Isaiah iv. 4:

> When the Lord shall have washed away the filth of the daughters of Zion, and shall have purged the blood of Jerusalem from the midst thereof, by the spirit of burning.

The design and end of the divine judgments is clearly expressed by this prophet, chap. xxvii. 9:

> By this, therefore, shall the iniquity of Jacob be purged; and this is all the fruit to take away his sin.

There is, perhaps, no passage of scripture on which more dependence is placed for proof positive of a state of punishment in a future world, and to all eternity, than the following: last paragraph of Luke xvi., verses 19-31:

> There was a certain rich man, which was clothed in purple and fine linen, and fared sumptuously every day: And there was a certain beggar named Lazarus, which was laid at his gate, full

of sores, And desiring to be fed with the crumbs which fell from the rich mans table: moreover the dogs came and licked his sores. And it came to pass, that the beggar died, and was carried by the angels into Abraham's bosom: the rich man also died, and was buried; And in hell he lift up his eyes, being in torments, and seeth Abraham afar off, and Lazarus in his bosom. And he cried and said, Father Abraham, have mercy on me, and send Lazarus, that he may dip the tip of his finger in water, and cool my tongue; for I am tormented in this flame. But Abraham said, Son, remember that thou in thy lifetime receivedst thy good things, and likewise Lazarus evil things: but now he is comforted, and thou art tormented. And beside all this, between us and you there is a great gulf fixed: so that they which would pass from hence to you cannot; neither can they pass to us, that would come from thence. Then he said, I pray thee therefore, father, that thou wouldest send him to my fathers house: For I have five brethren; that he may testify unto them, lest they also come into this place of torment. Abraham saith unto him, They have Moses and the prophets; let them hear them. And he said, Nay, father Abraham: but if one went unto them from the dead, they will repent. And he said unto him, If they hear not Moses and the prophets, neither will they be persuaded, though one rose from the dead.

In this parable, my opposers contend, we have a very plain and literal account of the death of a rich man, and of his being in hell after death; and the death of a poor man, and his future happiness. It is contended by the most of those who oppose the doctrine which we endeavor to vindicate that this paragraph ought to be taken and understood in its most literal sense, and that Christ did not intend it as a parable.

Though I am very far from believing this paragraph to be a literal account, yet I will admit it, for the better accommodation of the argument. For if I do not, but only give my opinion on the passage, my opponent will contend that the objection is not answered, as he rests it on the literality of the passage. Admitting the account just as literal as my opposer views it, is it possible for him to substantiate an objection against us from it? I think not; for, were it possible to prove that an individual who died in the days of Noah had continued from that time until now in a state of misery, it would have no force to prove that such individual would be miserable a single year longer, much less, to prove he would be endlessly so.

Further, could it be proved that a person who recently died would be in the worst of torments for a million of years to come, it would fall infinitely short of proving that he would suffer endlessly. If the suffering of a rational being for a time prove that this being must be endlessly miserable, the proof stands against the whole family of Adam, not excepting Jesus himself. If my opponent be under the necessity of giving me the argument in this particular, which I know he must, then what evidence has he left, in the scripture under consideration, to prove endless misery? If it be urged against me that the gulf between Abraham and the rich man was impassable, it proves nothing with regard to its duration.

Let us now examine the passage a little, taking notice of the common ideas of it. It is said that the rich man lifted up his eyes in hell. Now it is believed and argued that souls in hell are as destitute of any principle of goodness as the devil in which people believe; that they are folly engaged in the devil's service, and opposed to anything and all things which are favorable to the kingdom of the Savior. This being the case, how is it that we have such an account of the prayer which the rich man made to his father Abraham in favor of his five brethren? He seems to be anxious for their welfare, and desires that they might not come into such a place of torment as he was in. How would such a prayer please Beezlebub, the prince of devils? Did I believe in such a being, according to the general idea which people have of him, I should suppose he would be very much alarmed on hearing such benevolent prayers made in his dark dominions! The prayer seems to favor the plan of Gospel grace more than the vile purposes of Satan, though it did not seem to dictate the matter exactly according to the divine purpose. It is generally believed that the devil is desirous of getting as many as possible into misery; if so, and the rich man desired that his brethren might not come into that place of torment, let his reasons be what they might, it is evident that his desires were opposed to the devil's. "A kingdom, divided against itself, cannot stand." (Matt. xii. 25.)

Again, it is argued by some that those who are in heaven will rejoice in consequence of the misery of those whom they see in torment, as the justice of God will, by their torments, be made to appear more glorious than it otherwise could,— which, by the way, answers the most fervent desires of Satan. This being granted, should those who are in heaven, on seeing those in hell, who, in this world, were their nearest connections, feel the smallest regret, much more, desire to grant them assistance, it would be a complete violation of that justice which confined them there. But in our text, it is shown that those who are in Abraham's bosom are desirous of going to the rich man, and their object is plainly seen, that it is to relieve him from his torments, see Luke xiv. 26, "So that those who would pass from hence to you cannot." It is very evident that those who were in Abraham's bosom were desirous of assisting the rich man; and according to the common idea, it must have been deemed a rebellion against the will and justice of God, in consequence of which, if the devil deserved to be cast out of heaven for his disobedience, these undoubtedly deserved the same condemnation!

If we look impartially into these things, it is easy to see that something wrong has been entertained in the common idea. By a little attention to the introduction of this paragraph in Luke, the reader may easily see the whole was intended as a similitude, to show the adultery which the high priest would commit in rejecting the Gospel, and endeavoring to obtain justification by attending to the law in the letter; and also the situation of that part of Israel that was broken off through unbelief, which is represented by St. Paul, Rom. xi. 7-10:

> What then? Israel hath not obtained that which he seeketh for; but the election hath obtained it, and the rest were blinded. (According as it is written, God hath given them the spirit of slumber, eyes that they should not see, and ears that they should not hear;) unto this day. And David saith, let their table be made a snare, and a trap, and a stumbling-block, and a recompense unto them: let their eyes be darkened, that they may not see, and bow down their back alway.

See Matt. xxi. 43:

> Therefore say I unto you, the kingdom of God shall be taken from you, and given to a nation bringing forth the fruits thereof.

How evidently this agrees with the words of Abraham to the rich man in the parable (Luke xvi. 25):

> Son, remember that in thy life time thou hadst thy good things, and likewise Lazarus evil things: but now he is comforted, and thou art tormented.

Matt. xxi. 31:

> Jesus saith unto them, Verily I say unto you, that the publicans and harlots go into the kingdom of God before you.

Acts xiii. 45-47:

> But when the Jews saw the multitudes they were filled with envy, and spake against those things which were spoken by Paul, contradicting and blaspheming. Then Paul and Barnabas waxed bold, and said, it was necessary that the word of God should first have been spoken to you; but seeing ye put it from you, and judge yourselves unworthy of everlasting life, lo, we turn to the Gentiles; for so hath the Lord commanded us, saying, I have set thee to be a light of the Gentiles, that thou shouldst be for salvation unto the ends of the earth.

It seems, according to the scriptures, that it was so ordered, in the wisdom of God, that the Jews, who were his chosen people, should, through unbelief, be broken off from their own olive-tree, and that the Gentile church should be grafted in. See Rom. xi. 17, 24. This subject is, doubtless, that which the parable of the rich man and Lazarus was designed to represent. But that the Jews were broken off through unbelief, so that they were never to be grafted in again; or that their fall was such as to preclude recovery is certainly very fully refuted by the Apostle of the Gentiles, in the chapter to which we have before alluded. See Rom. xi. 11-12:

> I say then, have they stumbled that they should fall? God forbid; but rather through their fall salvation is come unto the Gentiles, for to provoke them to jealousy. Now if the fall of them be the riches of the world, and the diminishing of them the riches of the Gentiles; how much more their fullness.

Verse 15:

> For if the casting away of them be the reconciling of the world, what shall the receiving of them be but life from the dead?

See also the whole remainder of the chapter. But particularly notice verses 25-26:

> For I would not, brethren, that ye should be ignorant of this mystery, lest ye should be wise in your own conceit; that blindness in part is happened to Israel, until the fullness of the Gentiles be come in. And so all Israel shall be saved: as it is written, there shall come out of Zion the deliverer, and shall turn away ungodliness from Jacob!

Observe how the following passages correspond; one from the parable, the other from the history of the fact: Abraham says, "Besides all this, between us and you there is a great gulf fixed; so that they which would pass from hence to you cannot: neither can they pass to us that would come from thence." "Blindness in part is happened to Israel, until the fullness of the Gentiles be come in." This blindness which happened to Israel constituted, between them and Abraham's faith called in the parable his bosom, an impassable gulf. See John xii. 37-41:

> But though he had done so many miracles before them, yet they believed not on him; that the saying of Esaias the prophet might be fulfilled, which he spake, Lord, who hath believed

our report? And to whom hath the arm of the Lord been revealed? Therefore they could not believe, because that Esaias said again, he hath blinded their eyes, and hardened their heart, that they should not see with their eyes, nor understand with their heart, and be converted, and I should heal them. These things said Esaias when he saw his glory, and spake of him.

If my opposer contend that what I here call the parable of the rich man and Lazarus ought not to be called a parable, because it is not so called where it is recorded, I deem it sufficient that I refer to a passage which I will not hesitate to call a parable, but which is not said in the scripture where it occurs, to be a parable. See Judges ix. 8-15. The passage begins thus: "The trees went forth on a time to anoint a king over them; and they said unto the olive-tree, reign thou over us: The olive-tree refuses. They next apply to the fig-tree, and that refuses. They next apply to the vine, and the vine refuses. They at last all go to the bramble, where they succeed in obtaining a king.

If I am told that the cases are by no means parallel, because every body knows that trees never talked to each other, and that they never wanted a king to reign over them, I reply: these well known facts are no better known than it is known that the eyes of a dead man in the grave see nothing, and that his ears hear nothing, and that his tongue feels nothing, and that his lips say nothing. If my opposer says that the rich man was not in the grave, but in hell, he is informed that the word which is here rendered hell is the same word which is rendered grave: 1 Cor. xv. 55: "O death, where is thy sting? O grave, where is thy victory?" Now if he contend that this hell is a place of torment in the invisible world, he must grant that it will be overcome; for the apostle adds (verses 56-57),

> The sting of death is sin; and the strength of sin is the law. But thanks be to God which giveth us the victory through our Lord Jesus Christ.

But I would have it distinctly understood, that I do not believe that the parable has any reference to the state of man in the future world.

There is a passage in Matt. xii. 31-32 which has been contended for as an unanswerable objection to universal salvation. The text reads thus:

> Wherefore I say unto you, all manner of sin and blasphemy shall be forgiven unto men; but the blasphemy against the Holy Ghost shall not be forgiven unto men. And whosoever speaketh a word against the Son of man, it shall be forgiven him; but whosoever speaketh against the Holy Ghost, it shall not be forgiven him, neither in this world nor in the world to come.

The common idea of this world and the world to come is the present life of man on earth, and that state in which man exists here after. Could it be proved that this was the right meaning of the word "world," there would be something more in the text than we can now see. Some who have ably defended the doctrine of universal salvation have admitted the common idea of the passage, so far as it goes to prove future misery; yet have abundantly proved that it would come to an end. But if the word "world" have the signification of age or dispensation, as will not be disputed, it will be impossible to prove that anything beyond what may be experienced by men in this mortal state was intended in this text.

We are informed that Christ came once in the end of the world, to put away sin, by the sacrifice of himself. The world, in the end of which Christ came, was undoubtedly the dispensation of the legal priesthood; according to which idea, the world, which was then to come, is the dispensation of Gospel light which rose on the Gentile world, for the purpose of bringing them to the knowledge and worship of the true God; which dispensation ends with the conversion of the fullness of the Gentiles, and will be succeeded by that in which Israel will be visited by the spirit of their Messiah, and shall say, Blessed is he who cometh in the name of the Lord.

What I have written on this subject will show the reader the propriety of supposing that the sin which the Pharisees committed in blaspheming the Holy Spirit, by which Christ wrought miracles, has been visited upon their descendents even to this day, and will continue upon them until the fullness of the Gentiles be come in. But I see no need of carrying the meaning of these words to an endless eternity, or even beyond the experience of man in this natural life. Therefore, admitting the doctrine of future punishment true, I cannot see it proved from these words.

Could it be proved that eternal or endless misery was a natural production of the divine nature, there being an unchangeable principle to support such misery, the argument on my part must be given up. If sin be, in a moral sense, the cause of misery; should sin ever be brought to an end, its consequences, which are misery, would also come to an end. If my opponent can tell me how Jesus will finish sin, and make an end of transgression, and yet sin and transgression continue as long as God exists, he will embarrass me more than all his objections have been able to do.

10. Reasons for Believing in Universal Reconciliation

Having answered, as I hope to the reader's satisfaction, some of the most important objections against God's universal goodness to his creatures, I shall now turn on the other hand, and give the reader some of my evidences for believing in the so-much-despised doctrine of universal holiness and happiness.

First, I reason from the nature of divine goodness, in which all pretend to believe, and none dare in a direct sense to deny, that God could not, consistently with himself, create a being that would experience more misery than happiness. Secondly, if God be infinitely good, his goodness is commensurate with his power and knowledge; then all beings whom his power produced are the objects of his goodness; and to prove that any being was destitute of it would prove that Deity's knowledge did not comprehend such being. Thirdly, there is as much propriety in saying that God is infinite in power but that he did not create all things, as there is in saying though God be infinite in goodness, yet part of his creatures will never be the partakers of it. It might as well be said that God is infinite in knowledge and yet ignorant of the most part of events which are daily and hourly taking place, as to say that he is infinitely good and yet only a few of his creatures were designed for happiness. Fourthly, if the Almighty, as we believe him to be, did not possess power sufficient to make all his creatures happy, it was not an act of goodness in him to create them. If he have that power, but possess no will for it, it makes a bad matter as much worse as is possible. I then reduce my opponent to the necessity of telling me if those whom he believes will be endlessly lost, be those whom God could save, but would not, or those whom he would save, but could not. If it be granted that God has both power and will to save all men, it is granting all I want for a foundation of my faith.

I would further argue that as man is constituted to enjoy happiness on moral principles (to the knowledge of which principles we come by degrees), it is as reasonable to believe that all men were intended to obtain a consummate knowledge of the moral principles of their nature as that any of Adam's race were. There is not an individual of the whole family of man who is perfectly satisfied with those enjoyments which earth and time afford him; the soul is constituted for nobler pleasures, which to me is an evidence that God has provided for all men some better things than can be found in earthly enjoyments, where we find but little except vanity and disappointment. There is an immortal desire in every soul for future existence and happiness. For the truth of this assertion I appeal to the consciences of my readers. Why should the Almighty implant this desire in us if he never intended to satisfy it? Supposing a mother has the power of modifying the desires and appetite of her child, would she cause it to want that which she could not get for it? Would she take pleasure in seeing her child pine for fruits which did not grow in the country where she lived, and which she could not get? Or would she prefer the anguish of the child to its happiness, when it was in her power to grant all it wanted? If such a mother were to be found, who would call her a godly woman? Could her child, thus tormented, rise up and call her blessed? No, surely it could not.

I further argue that all wise, good, and exemplary men wish for the truth of the doctrine for which I contend; they earnestly pray for the salvation of all men, and do all in their power, by the grace of God, to dissuade men from sin, to the obedience of the Gospel; they enlist willingly into the service of virtue, to endeavor to win proselytes to holiness; their object is the destruction of sin, and the advancement of righteousness, and they believe, and I think justly, that God will bless their labors.

None but wicked men would wish for the endless duration of sin. Were it left to the carnal mind, it would wish for nothing but the privilege of drinking in iniquity forever. But those who truly love God and holiness desire night and day to overcome the vile propensities of their own deceitful hearts, and pray for the reconciliation of others to holiness and happiness. Now, why should we suppose that God is more of the mind of the wicked than of the righteous? If it be God's spirit in us which causes us to pray for the destruction of sin, is it reasonable to say that this same spirit has determined that sin shall always exist? Are we not right in judging of the nature and character of God from the dictates of his spirit in us? If so, does this spirit teach us the necessity of endless transgression and misery? I wish the reader to keep in mind that I hold sin and misery inseparably connected, and holiness and happiness so likewise.

I further argue, if any of the human race be endlessly miserable, the whole must be, providing they all know it; for, reasoning from that spirit of benevolence which is necessary to a conformity to the principles of holiness, I prove it impossible for a well-disposed man to see another in misery without bearing a very sensible proportion of such misery. If it be argued that this idea is wrong, and that the spirit which dictates it is of the evil one; I say, in answer, all good men in the world feel it to be a truth; and no man ever exhibited more of it than the Savior of the world.

If anyone should be so particular as to query, asking if the Almighty himself be not desirous of the salvation of sinners; and if so, how can this happiness be complete? I answer, a being to whom events do not take place in succession, nor time pass away, with whom an eternity is a present now, whose knowledge is intuitive, and who can neither hope nor anticipate, can neither increase nor decrease in happiness. But when we speak of God, abstractedly, our words ought to be few and chosen.

Those who are the most devout on earth are the most desirous for the advancement of the Redeemer's kingdom, and the deliverance of themselves and their fellow-men by sin, from sin and misery. For the sake of a case, I will suppose a Christian today is exercised with fervent desires for the reconciliation of sinners; at night, he dies. Do all those holy desires cease at death? If they do not, but do continue, though the happiness of the soul be great, yet it is, at least, capable of being enlarged, or increased, by the prosperity of the Redeemer's cause among men.

How the idea ever got place in the human mind, that even fathers and mothers, in the world to come, would rejoice to see their own offspring in endless flames and hopeless torments, I can hardly conceive; though the probability is, it was first invented to shun, in theory, those difficulties not otherwise to be avoided. I wish to use this error as prudently as possible; but I wish to have it rightfully understood, and judged of impartially. Will perfect reconciliation to God have this effect? I know it is contended that it will; but what evidence have we of it? Was not Christ reconciled, or in a state of conformity to God's law? Did he manifest joy at the sufferings of mankind? When he looked on Jerusalem, that abominable city, and knew that its chiefs would be his murderers, when he spake of the dreadful calamities just ready to burst on their devoted heads, how did he feel? Streams of sorrow broke from the eye of innocence; in his grief, he spake of their destruction, but prophesies of seeing him again, when they should welcome him, saying, "Blessed is he that cometh in the name of the Lord!" (Psa. cxviii. 26; Matt. xxi. 9.)

If perfect reconciliation to God will effect complete happiness at the sight of human misery, the more we are reconciled to God the more satisfaction we should take in seeing our fellow-creatures miserable! Then, those who can look on men in distress with the least sorrow are the most reconciled to divine goodness; and those who feel the most sorrow at the afflictions of their fellow-men are the most perverse and wicked! Some may say, heaven is entirely different from this world, and when we get there we shall be totally changed from what we now are; therefore, it will not do to argue what we shall be there from what we ought to be here. Then the awful fact is, all we call goodness here will be called badness there; and that which we call badness here will be goodness there!

If the effects of moral holiness in the world to come should be different from what they are here, I wish to be informed on what moral principle the change is made. If these things be so, the souls of the cruel need but little alteration to prepare them for heaven, and that little laid out in making them what we should call worse. Such a heaven as this does not, I hope, exist in the universe. My opponent will urge his argument still further on this subject, and say, it is not the misery of the wicked that affords so much pleasure to those who are in heaven, but their joy is increased in consequence of the execution of justice. This, however, is giving up what is contended for, namely, that every degree of misery will create thousands of degrees of happiness; because, could divine justice be as well understood without this misery as with it, the misery itself would do no good.

I am willing to grant that a good man will prefer the execution of justice to his own private ease, or the partial happiness of a criminal. But how would a judge appear who should manifest joy and gladness on pronouncing the sentence of death upon one of his fellow-men? Who would not turn from such a court with disgust and deep abhorrence? To call such a circumstance an instance in which men have an occasion to rejoice is a violation of our senses.

I will say for myself, I neither expect nor desire perfect happiness while I see my fellow-men in misery; I had rather be possessed of that sympathy which causes me to feel for another than to enjoy an unsocial pleasure in a frosty heaven of misanthropy. Is it possible that we should be completely happy and see those in misery whom we love? No one will say we can. Are we not commanded to love our enemies? Can we be truly happy and not love them? Surely we cannot; then how can we be completely happy and see them miserable?

A parent may be persuaded to attend his child while a surgeon performs an amputation; but with what acute feelings his heart is agitated! How eagerly would he inhale the pain and make it his own were it possible! But there is something in all this that is tolerable; he is in hopes of saving the life of his child: were it not for his hopes, could he endure the sight? But what is all this compared with a parent viewing his child in endless flames! O parents, what a blessed circumstance it is that when we are called to part with our children on earth, we can mingle a little joy with the sorrow in hoping that they belong to the deathless family in heaven!

If the good desires which are found in the Christian heart are ever to be satisfied, universal subjection to the government of Christ will surely take place; if virtue ever gains an universal victory over sin and vice, universal holiness and happiness will be the consequence. Man exists on such a principle as renders him capable of improving in knowledge and happiness, which he obtains by experience; and it is very evident that as the wheels of time move, man is fast advancing, which favors the idea that at some period known to Deity, the desired haven will be obtained in the acquisition of that wisdom which is from above.

When we send our children to school it is for the purpose of learning that of which they are ignorant; and it is by degrees that those sciences are obtained which constitute them learned. When a child first takes a quill in hand to write, he blunders, but does not blunder so as to imitate the copy; neither will two out of a thousand imitate each other.

Men begin their moral existence in their separate capacity in the same way; unacquainted with the skill of their divine preceptor, they err from sacred rules and differ from their fellow-pupils. Jars and broils ensue, and sorrow and woe are the consequences. But as they become taught, they conform to the divine rules of their master and learn that their happiness consists in being united.

Happiness is the greatest object of all rational beings, and no one will follow any particular object any longer than he thinks it subservient to his main one. The reason why men sin is, they think, and think erroneously, that they shall obtain more happiness in so doing than in following the dictates of truth. But is it reasonable to suppose that the error will never be discovered? Will the sinner never find his mistake? O yes, says my opposer, to his eternal confusion and endless misery! But stop a moment; if he find his mistake he will abandon the object; and when he ceases to sin he begins to reform and approximate towards holiness and happiness.

I have sufficiently argued that man cannot be miserable in consequence of moral condemnation any longer than he is, in a moral sense, a sinner. Then he must sin endlessly in order to be miserable so long; which if so, he will never find his mistake, he will never learn that righteousness and truth are more productive of happiness than sin. But I think it erroneous to suppose that a being who is capable of learning anything cannot learn some time short of eternity that it is better to do right than wrong. Should we argue, however, that that might in some cases be true, it would destroy the idea of complete and positive misery for which my opponent contends. Complete misery would not admit of a prospect which could administer the smallest hope; in which case, the soul would have no object which could possibly induce it to action; then would the soul become inert, and its existence would be destroyed, and become not a subject of happiness or misery.

I would argue again, from a reasonable idea admitted by all, namely, that mankind in their moral existence originated in God. Why, then, do we deny man's final assimilation with the fountain from whence he sprang? The streams and rivulets which water the hill-country run in every direction, as the make of land occasions. They are stained with various mines and soils through which they pass; but at last they find their entrance into the ocean, where their different courses are at an end, and they are tempered like the fountain which receives them. Though man, at present, forms an aspect similar to the waters in their various courses, yet in the end of his race I hope he will enjoy an union with his God, and with his fellows.

Having given a few hints, from the nature of moral beings, in favor of my general plan, I shall beg the attention of the reader to some evidences, from the Scriptures of truth, in favor of universal holiness and happiness. The method I intend to pursue will be conclusive; for I am determined to admit no Scripture as evidence, in this case, that needs any interpretation to cause it to mean what I wish to prove; therefore I shall produce but a small part of the Scriptures which I conceive have a direct meaning in favor of Universalism.

It will not be expected that all, or more than a small part of the passages, which relate to this subject will be presented in this work; but I will endeavor to arrange those I do adduce in such order, and accompany them with such remarks, as I hope may convey conviction to the candid reader.

It is well known that the gospel dispensation is intimately connected with certain promises which God made to the ancient fathers of the Jewish nation. See Gal. iii. 16-18:

> Now to Abraham and to his seed were the promises made. He saith not, and to seeds, as of many; but as of one, and to thy seed, which is Christ. And this I say, that the covenant that was confirmed before of God in Christ, the law, which was four hundred and thirty years after, cannot disannul, that it should make the promise of none effect. For if the inheritance be of the law, it is no more of promise, but God gave it to Abraham by promise.

Heb. vi. 17-20:

> Wherein God willing more abundantly to show unto the heirs of promise the immutability of his counsel, confirmed it by an oath; that by two immutable things, in which it was impossible for God to lie, we might have strong consolation, who have fled for refuge, to lay hold upon the hope set before us: which

hope we have as an anchor of the soul both sure and steadfast, and which entereth into that within the veil; whither the forerunner is for us entered, even Jesus made an high priest forever, after the order of Melchisedec.

Acts xiii. 30-33:

But God raised him from the dead; and he was seen many days of them which came up with him from Galilee to Jerusalem, who are his witnesses unto the people. And we declare unto you glad tidings, how that the promise which was made unto the fathers, God hath fulfilled the same unto us their children, in that he hath raised up Jesus again.

We presume it is not necessary to quote more passages to show that the gospel of Jesus Christ, with all its favors, is pursuant to certain promises which God made to the fathers. This fact being clearly understood, it will appear altogether reasonable that we begin our examination of scripture proof of whatever we believe in, as the final result of the gospel schemes, by a careful examination of those primitive promises; for if, as we have seen in the passage just quoted from Acts, the glad tidings of the gospel proclaimed by the apostle, were a declaration that the promise which God made to the fathers he had fulfilled the same by raising up Jesus again, then have we a right to believe in all that we find contained in the promises and nothing more.

Now as we are going to examine those ancient promises of our heavenly Father, and as we are about to inquire into their most evident import in reference to what we ought to believe will be the final result of the gospel of Jesus Christ, let us engage in this work with honest unprejudiced minds; and let us lay aside all prepossessions which might tend to bias our judgment and be willing to submit to whatever we find in this great charter of the divine will. See Gen. xii. 1-3:

Now the Lord had said unto Abraham, get thee out of thy country, and from thy kindred, and from thy father's house, unto a land that I will show thee, and I will make of thee a great nation, and I will bless thee, and make thy name great, and thou shalt be a blessing. And I will bless them that bless thee and curse him that curseth thee; and in thee shall all the families of the earth be blessed.

Chap. xxii. 15-18:

And the angel of the Lord called unto Abraham out of heaven the second time, and said, by myself have I sworn, saith the Lord, for because thou hast done this thing, and hast not withheld thy son, thine only son, that in blessing I will bless thee, and in multiplying I will multiply thy seed as the stars of the heaven, and as the sand which is upon the sea shore; and thy seed shall possess the gate of his enemies: and in thy seed shall all the nations of the earth be blessed.

This promise which God made to Abraham, he confirmed to Isaac, as we read in chap. xxvi. 3-4:

Sojourn in this land; and I will be with thee, and will bless thee; for unto thee and to thy seed 1 will give all these countries; and I will perform the oath which I sware unto Abraham thy father; and I will make thy seed to multiply as the stars of heaven, and will give unto thy seed all these countries; and in thy seed shall all the nations of the earth be blessed.

See also the confirmation of this promise to Jacob: chap. xviii. 13-14:

And, behold, the Lord stood above it, and said, I am the Lord God of Abraham thy father, and the God of Isaac: the land whereon thou liest, to thee will I give it, and to thy seed, and thy seed shall be as the dust of the earth; and thou shalt spread abroad to the west, and to the east, and to the north, and to the south; and in thee, and in thy seed, shall all the families of the earth be blessed.

Having these promises thus before us, it may be of service to notice several particulars in their character. First: As to the blessing or blessings which they promise to all the nations and to all the families of the earth, there appears an entire impartiality. Second: Whatever blessing or blessings were intended by these promises, there is not the least intimation that they were promised on any conditionality. That the fulfillment of them depended entirely on the will and power of God is seen by the passage before quoted from Acts xiii. 32-33:

> And we declare unto you glad tidings, how that the promise which was made unto the fathers, God hath fulfilled the same unto us their children, in that he hath raised up Jesus again.

It seems, according to this very plain testimony, that the resurrection of Jesus was the fulfillment of the promise to bless all the nations and all the families of the earth in the seed of Abraham, Isaac, and Jacob, which seed is Christ.

Now that there may be no mistake or doubt as to what the blessing is which was promised to all the nations and to all the families of the earth in Christ, we invite the reader's attention to the following scriptures: Gal. iii. 8:

> And the scriptures, foreseeing that God would justify the heathen through faith, preached before the gospel unto Abraham, saying, in thee shall all nations be blest.

By this passage we learn that the blessing promised was justification through faith. Compare Rom. iv. 25:

> Who was delivered for our offences, and was raised again for our justification.

See more corresponding passages: Col. i. 20:

> And, (having made peace by the blood of his cross) by him to reconcile all things unto himself; by him, I say, whether they be things in earth, or things in heaven.

That the things to be reconciled were man may be seen next by the next verse:

> And you, that were sometime alienated, and enemies in your minds by wicked works, yet now hath he reconciled.

The way in which Christ effected this reconciliation is expressed in the next verse:

> In the body of his flesh through death to present you holy, and unblameable, and unprovable in his sight.

Eph. i. 9-10:

Having made known unto us the mystery of his will, according to his good pleasure, which he hath prepared in himself: that, in the dispensation of the fullness of times he might gather together in one all things in Christ, both which are in heaven, and which are on earth; even in him.

What a glorious foundation for hope is here. How blessed was Abraham when he rejoiced in the day of Jesus. How blessed were the prophets of the Lord who saw these things, though afar off; the sight weaned their affections from all earthly things; they sought a city which hath foundation, whose builder and maker is God. When Jacob blessed his sons, he spake of the coming of Shiloh, unto whom, saith he, shall the gathering of the people be; see Genesis xlix. 10; how exactly does this testimony of the patriarch agree with that of the apostle's:

Unto him shall the gathering of the people be.

And the apostle's testimony (Eph. i. 10):

That in the dispensation of the fullness of times, he might gather together in one all things in Christ.

We will hear what the prophet David, says, concerning the kingdom of Christ, Psalms lxxii. 11:

Yea, all kings shall fall down before him; all nations shall serve him.

Verse 1:

He shall redeem their soul from deceit and violence.

Verse 17:

And men shall be blessed in him, all nations shall call him blessed.

If any wish to argue that David meant no other than Solomon by the King's son, let them take notice of the 7th and 8th verses:

In his days shall the righteous flourish; and abundance of peace so long as the moon endureth. He shall have dominion also from sea to sea, and from the river unto the ends of the earth.

The moon yet endures, but the reign of Solomon does not. The kingdom spoken of in the text was to be universal; but Solomon's was not. Let us take particular notice of the 11th verse:

> Yea all kings shall fall down before him.

Shall all the cruel tyrants of the earth bow down to him who was born in a stable? Shall all the haughty kings of the proud and wealthy nations, bow down to him whose chosen companions when on earth were poor fishermen? Will you, our opponent, say, this is a pleasing doctrine to the carnal mind? Herod, who caused the massacre in Bethlehem in order to murder Christ in infancy, could hardly be persuaded that it was agreeable to his carnal mind to bow before Jesus at the head of this little band of martyrs. No, carnal mind must be crucified before all this can be done.

Would it please the present kings of Europe to tell them to beat their swords into ploughshares, and their spears into pruning hooks, and to learn war no more? Would it be agreeable to their carnal, proud, and haughty minds to submit to the religion of their Savior? Which of them would, in order to gratify carnal-mindedness, abandon all his equipage, his horses and chariots of state, mount a forlorn ass, ride into an enemy's land, preach peace and salvation to his inveterate foes, and pray for his murderers in death? And can you believe that *all* the kings of the earth can bow down before the Savior, with any more gratification to carnal-mindedness, than they could imitate him in his life and death?

"All nations shall serve him." (Psa. lxxii. 11.) If all nations serve Christ, will they not all be blessed in him according to the promise? I do not argue that any will be blessed in Christ who do not serve him; but the text says all nations shall serve him. Psa. xxxvii. 10:

> For yet a little while, and the wicked shall not be, yea, thou shalt diligently consider his place, and it shall not be.

Verse 36:

> Yet he passed away, and he was not, yes I sought him, but he could not be found.

If the wicked continue in sin as long as God exists, it appears to me to be improper to say, "Yet a little while, and the wicked shall not be." And if God has prepared a place of endless torments for the wicked, and that in sight of the righteous in heaven, it is hardly proper to say, "Thou shalt diligently consider his place, and it shall not be." And if the wicked are to be tormented forever in sight of the righteous, why is it said, "I sought him but he could not be found"? (Psa. xxii. 27.) Then see Psa. xxii. 27:

> All the ends of the world shall remember and turn unto the Lord, and all the kindred of the nations shall worship before thee.

Who will doubt the salvation of those who turn unto the Lord and worship before him? See Psa. ii. 7-8:

> I will declare the decree: the Lord hath said unto me, thou art my Son; this day have I begotten thee. Ask of me, and I shall give thee the heathen for thine inheritance, and the uttermost parts of the earth for thy possession.

Compare this beautiful passage with one like it in Col. i. 19:

> For it pleased the Father that in him should all fullness dwell.

In what a capacious Savior did David believe! Should a preacher at the present day recite the words which I have just quoted he would immediately be accused of holding the heretical doctrine of universal salvation, as his hearers might be pleased to call it; or should he communicate the doctrine half as clearly as it is communicated in those quotations, that part of his audience who were warmly opposed to the doctrine would grow uneasy, while those who favored the doctrine would be satisfied their speaker did so likewise. Some method must be used to explain those Scriptures differently from what they say, or the doctrine for which I contend is fairly proved by them.

Let us pass to the prophecies of Isaiah; see chap. xxv. 6-8:
> And in this mountain shall the Lord of hosts make unto all people a feast of fat things, a feast of wines on the lees, of fat

> things full of marrow, of wines on the lees well refined. And he will destroy in this mountain the face of the covering cast over all people, and the veil that is spread over all the nations. He will swallow up death in victory; and the Lord God will wipe away tears from off all faces; and the rebuke of his people shall be taken from off all the earth: for the Lord hath spoken it.

No one will doubt that the provisions here spoken of are those which are provided in the Gospel of salvation.

In the first place, then, observe it is made for all people; this proves that it was the intention of him who made the feast that all people should share in its divine benefits.

Secondly: It is testified that the veil of darkness which was over all people shall finally be taken away.

Thirdly: That death is to be swallowed up in victory, and tears wiped away from off all faces. And,

Lastly: That the rebuke of God's people should be taken from off all the earth. And the evidence given to prove it all would be done is, the Lord hath spoken it.

It is of no avail for any to pretend that though the provisions of the Gospel were provided for all people, yet all will not partake of them, let the reasons be what they may; for if God wipe tears from off all faces, all must receive the benefits of Gospel grace and peace. Compare this testimony with 1 Cor. xv. 54:

> So when this corruptible shall have put on incorruption, and this mortal shall put on immortality, then shall be brought to pass the saying that is written, death is swallowed up in victory.

Again, with Rev. xxi. 4:

> And God shall wipe away all tears from their eyes, and there shall be no more death, neither sorrow nor crying, neither shall there be any more pain: for the former things are passed away.

How can it be justly said that death is swallowed up in victory when the fact is death will reign as long as God exists? Or, how can it be said that God shall wipe away all tears from the eyes of men, if millions are to mourn to an endless eternity? Or, why is it said there shall be no more sorrow, crying nor pain, if sorrow, crying and infinite pain are never to come? In Isaiah ix. 6-7, the Savior is prophesied of as possessing a kingdom, the increase of which should have no end. To the same purpose, see also Daniel vii. 14:

> And there was given him dominion, and glory, and a kingdom, that all people, nations, and languages, should serve him; his dominion is an everlasting dominion, which shall not pass away, and his kingdom that which shall not be destroyed.

Observe, "*All* people, nations, and languages shall serve him." If a great part of the human race are to exist in endless rebellion against Christ and his kingdom, it seems that the prophet was not only ignorant of it but believed the reverse. See Isaiah xlix. 6:

> And he said, it is a light thing that thou shouldst be my servant, to raise up the tribes of Jacob, and to restore the preserved of Israel: I will also give thee for a light to the Gentiles, that thou mayest be my salvation unto the ends of the earth.

Verse 8:

> I will preserve thee, and give thee for a covenant of the people, etc.

For the strength of this covenant, see Jer. xxxiii. 20:

> Thus saith the Lord; if ye can break my covenant of the day, and my covenant of the night, and that there should not be day and night in their season; then may also my covenant be broken with David my servant, etc.

When men are possessed of sufficient agency to stop the wheels of time, to silence the motion of the solar system, and to disannul God's covenant with day and night, then day and night will depend on the will of man. So likewise, when he has agency to disannul that covenant which is ordered, and in all things sure, then his eternal salvation will depend on himself, and not on his God.

Attend to the similitude of the Redeemer's glory, from the

prophecy of Ezek. xvii., last paragraph (verses 22-24):
> Thus saith the Lord God, I will also take of the highest branch of the high cedar, and will set it; I will crop off from the top of his young twigs a tender one, and will plant it upon a high mountain and eminent: in the mountain of the height of Israel will I plant it: and it shall bring forth boughs and bear fruit and be a goodly cedar; and under it shall dwell all fowl of every wing; in the shadow of the branches thereof shall they dwell. And all the trees of the field shall know that I the Lord have brought down the high tree, and have made the dry tree to flourish: I the Lord have spoken, and have done it.

Time would fail me to write one-half that might be quoted from prophets on this subject. I ask for no explanation on their testimony; if what they say do not prove my doctrine, I will not have recourse to explanations.

I have reasoned from the goodness of God to prove that it is his will that all men should finally be holy and happy; I will now call proof from divine revelation to the same idea. See St. Paul's 1st Epistle to Timothy, ii. 4:
> Who will have all men to be saved, and to come unto the knowledge of the truth.

What could induce St. Paul to write this sentence if he did not believe it? My opponent will say he believes it himself. Then, I say, all for which I argue is granted. But my opponent has a method by which he can explain this passage so that it may be true, and yet God may will the endless misery of millions. It is only to say that the passage is expressive of God's revealed will, but not of his secret will, arguing that his revealed will is in direct opposition to a will which he has seen fit not to reveal!

Though much use is made of this method in order to shun the force of this passage and many others, if there be any propriety in it, it is out of my sight; or if it would not betray a want of good sense in any other case, I will leave my reader to judge.

To say God's revealed will is contrary to his eternal and unrevealed will, would in me be blasphemy of the first magnitude; yet I do not doubt the sincerity of those who frequently say it. But is it not in a direct sense charging God with hypocrisy? However shocking it may seem, I know of no other light in which to view it.

Again, if God have a will which he has not revealed, and my opponent knows what it is, I would ask how he came by this knowledge? God's revealed will is that all men should be saved, but his secret will is that most of them should be eternally miserable! I would ask when this will was a secret? It has been openly talked of by limitarians ever since the light of the Gospel advanced so as to discover the apostasy of Christians.

St. Paul speaks of the mystery of God's will which he proposed in himself, which the apostle says God has made known. See Eph. i. 9:

Having made known unto us the mystery of his will, according to his good pleasure, which he purposed in himself.

And in verse 10 he tells what this will is, but it is very different from what my opposer says the hidden will of God is:

That in the dispensation of the fullness of times he might gather together in one all things in Christ, both which are in Heaven and which are on earth, even in him.

St. Peter says God is not willing that any should perish, but that all should come unto repentance. (2 Pet. iii. 9.)

In short, I cannot see the propriety of saying that God will have all men to be saved, and to come unto the knowledge of the truth, if he predestinated from all eternity millions for eternal misery; and if he created any to glorify him in endless torments, I cannot see why he should not be willing for them to perish, and answer the end for which he made them.

Again, what is that truth which God wills all men to know? According to the words of the text, it must be a truth consonant to their salvation, or they could not be saved and yet believe the truth. For instance, suppose out of the whole alphabet all are to endlessly miserable except the vowel letters, and the whole alphabet was brought to the knowledge of the truth; surely the vowels would believe they were to be saved, but all the consonants would believe they were going into endless torments; and the faith of the consonants would be as true a faith as that of the vowels. But how could the consonants enjoy salvation while possessing this faith?

There are some who do not admit my general system, but who will admit this part of it: namely, that it is the will of God that all men should finally be holy and happy, but say at the same time that it depends on the creature's accepting of offered mercy on the rational conditions of Gospel obedience, making Gospel obedience a prerequisite to salvation; while I contend that Gospel obedience is, in fact, Gospel salvation.

To be saved from sin is surely Gospel salvation, and to be obedient according to the dictates of Gospel grace, is salvation from sin. There is just as much propriety in making obedience a condition on which salvation is granted as there would be for a physician to propose to a patient in a fit of the asthma that he would afford relief on condition the patient should first breathe easily. However, if it be granted that it is God's will that all men should be finally holy and happy, I will more directly answer the supposition that this will may fail by the words of St. Paul. See Eph. i. 11:

> In whom we also have obtained an inheritance, being predestinated, according to the purpose of him who worketh all things after the counsel of his own will.

If God will have all men to be saved, and worketh all things after the counsel of his own will, it proves that for which I contend as fully as anything can be proved from Scripture. My opponent, perhaps, will say (as many have said to me in conversation) after meeting with much difficulty in arguing, "Anything may be proved by scripture." To which I reply there is one thing that the scriptures do not prove, neither can all the ingenuity of man make them substantiate it, and that is, the endless misery of a moral being.

If any of my opposers can prove, by scripture, the endless duration of sin and misery as plainly as the two passages above recited prove universal holiness and happiness, I will never contend any more on the subject.

I will take further notice of Paul's first communication to Timothy. He goes on, in the 5th and 6th verses, to give Timothy a reason for what he had asserted (1 Tim. ii. 5-6):

> For there is one God, and one Mediator between God and men, the man Christ Jesus, who gave himself a ransom for all, to be testified in due time.

The apostle's reasoning is evidently good and plain; for God would not have given his Son a ransom for all, if it were not his will that all should be saved; and if it be God's will it ought to be ours, therefore it is right to pray for all. If the ransom were paid for all, it argues that it was the intention of the Ransomer that all should be benefitted.

What would have been the astonishment of the world, after the immortal Washington had caused to be paid a ransom for all the American prisoners who were in Algerine slavery, if he had told the Dey that he did not want more than one quarter of those captives sent home to the land of liberty and to the enjoyment of their families for which they had so long sighed in bondage; and that he might wear out the rest with fatigue and whips? But the good man's soul was never satisfied until they all came home, and with songs of joyous liberty hailed the land of their nativity! And blessed be the Captain of our salvation; he, also, shall see of the travail of his soul and be satisfied, when all the "ransomed of the Lord shall return and come to Zion with songs and everlasting joys upon their heads, when they shall obtain joy and gladness, and sorrow and sighing shall flee away." (Isa. xxxv. 10.)

The reader's attention is now invited to those Scriptures

which, in expression, are more particularly applicable to the deliverance of mankind from this bondage of corruption into the glorious liberty of the children of God.

The whole of the 15th chapter of the 1st Epistle to the Corinthians was intended to refute those who denied the resurrection; but as that doctrine in not denied by my opponent, I shall take notice only of those parts which affect the argument between us. See verse 20:

> But now is Christ risen from the dead, and become the first fruits of them that slept.

Christ, as the first fruits of them who slept, is represented by the heave-offering under the law. See Num. xv. 19, 20:

> Then it shall be that, when ye eat of the bread of the land, ye shall offer up an heave-offering unto the Lord. Ye shall offer up a cake of the first of your dough, for an heave-offering: as ye do the heave-offering of the threshing-floor, so shall ye heave it.

Exod. xxii. 29:

> Thou shalt not delay to offer the first of thy ripe fruits, and of thy liquors; the first born of thy sons shalt thou give unto me.

See also Num. xviii. 15. By the offering of the first ripe fruits, the whole of the succeeding harvest was sanctified; and in the first born which were redeemed, the succeeding fruits of the womb were considered holy; see Acts xxvi. 23:

> That Christ should suffer, and that he should be the first that should rise from the dead.

Christ being the first who rose from the dead, and rising as the first fruits, sanctifies all the rest, as did the first fruits under the law. St. Paul's comment on the first fruits is very illustrative of the scriptural meaning thereof. See Rom. ix. 16:

> For if the first fruits be holy, so are the branches.

In the heave-offering under the law there is a beautiful representation of our Savior. The sheaf taken from the field, being separated from all the rest of the same growth, represents the separation of Jesus Christ from mankind to be holy unto the Lord; and the sanctification of the whole harvest, being by the first ripe fruits, is to show us that our sanctification is in Jesus, the first fruits of them that slept. The same may be clearly seen in the instance of the dough; a certain part of it was to be separated from the rest for an offering unto the Lord in which the remaining part of the lump (as the apostle calls it) was considered holy.

These observations are made here in order to draw the reader's attention more closely to the labors of the apostle which we have now under consideration (1 Cor. xv); for he goes on immediately to show what he means by the lump spoken of in Romans. See verse 21:

For since by man came death, by man came also the resurrection of the dead.

Let me here observe that death came by the earthly man, and the resurrection came by the heavenly man, which is in point to prove that the plan of the Gospel is to deliver mankind from the earthly Adam to the immortality of heaven.

Perhaps none would dispute what I here contend for, provided I did not extend the cure as extensively as the malady; but I shall also contend for this, and will clearly prove it by the apostle's testimony. See 1 Cor. xv. 22:

For as in Adam all die, even so in Christ shall all be made alive.

It is not possible for me to state the doctrine more concise and positive than the apostle has done so in the passage quoted. But I am willing to attend to my opponent's objections as I proceed. He will say he does not dispute that the apostle here meant all mankind, but that he only intended they would all be raised from the dead, not that all would be delivered from condemnation and sin. But I will rest my argument on the words themselves; I say, if all men are made alive in Christ, they cannot be said to be out of Christ dead or alive, sinful or holy.

The present state of our being is derived from Adam, the earthly nature; and, in a natural sense, we are all in him. Our future state of existence we derive entirely from the heavenly nature; and, therefore, it is said all shall be made alive in Christ. The apostle goes on still further to show the order of the beforementioned work, arguing, from the first fruits the whole family of mankind. See 1 Cor. xv. 23-25:

> But every man in his own order: Christ the first fruits; afterwards that that are Christ's at his coming. Then cometh the end, when he shall have delivered up the kingdom to God, even the Father: when he shall have put down all rule, and all authority and power. For he must reign till he hath put all enemies under his feet.

Christ is here again spoken of as the first fruits, in the order of the resurrection, which consists of three parts.

First, of Christ himself, who was the first that rose from the dead.

Secondly: Those who are Christ's at his coming, at what the apostle calls the end, which cannot be, until he hath put down all rule authority, and power, and every enemy has submitted; at which time, the Mediator delivers up the kingdom to God, the Father.

Then shall the great work of reconciliation be finished, and the labors of the Redeemer completed with immortal honor. Then shall *all* the millions of the human race be reconciled to God through Christ, and shall sing; see Rev. v. 11-14:

> And I beheld, and I heard the voice of many angels round about the throne, and the beasts, and the elders: and the number of them was ten thousand times ten thousand, and thousands of thousands; singing with a loud voice, Worthy is the Lamb that was slain, to receive power, and riches, and wisdom, and strength, and honor, and glory, and blessings. And every creature which is in heaven, and on the earth, and under the earth, and such as are in the sea, and all that are in them, heard I, saying, Blessing, and honor, and glory, and power, be unto him that sitteth upon the throne, and unto the Lamb, forever and ever. And the fours beasts said, amen. And the four and twenty elders fell down, and worshipped him that liveth for-

ever and ever.

The reader will observe that ten thousand times ten thousand, and thousands of thousands of angels, beasts and elders, first declare the Lamb, who had been slain, to be worthy to receive power, and riches, and wisdom, and strength, and honor, and glory, and blessings; then every creature which is in heaven, and on the earth, and under the earth, and such as are in the sea, and all that are in them, say: Blessing, and honor, and glory, and power, be unto him who sitteth upon the throne, and unto the Lamb forever and ever. Then the elders and beasts, who first pronounced him thus worthy, fell down and worshipped him who liveth forever and ever.

There is nothing in all the sacred writings more astonishingly beautiful than this account; neither do I think it possible for the imagination to paint anything half so grand and sublime. I am all astonishment! To realize by faith the accomplishment of this glorious prediction transcends every other thought or idea of which the mind is susceptible.

There is no room for my opponent to argue against the doctrine of universal holiness and happiness while this passage of divine truth lies in sight. There are no expressions left out of this passage that would make it more extensive.

May I not ask the opposer if he be not willing to acknowledge what mysterious powers have acknowledged, that Christ, the dear Lamb who hath been slain, is worthy to receive as extensive worship as is declared in the passage quoted?

When the four beasts and the elders saw universal nature bending before the object of their worship, they immediately fell down, anxious to excel, and worshipped him who liveth forever and ever. If my opponent thinks Christ is not worthy of so much worship, he thinks less of him than I do, and less than I wish he did.

There are yet remaining many passages in the 15th of 1st Corinthians which are in point to prove what I am contending for, even more than is at this time necessary to introduce. A few more, however, may be proper, with some few remarks. See verse 28:

> And when all things shall be subdued unto him, then shall the Son also himself be subject to him that did put all things under him, that God may be all in all.

What must we understand by all things being subdued unto him? Will any one say all that is meant by it, is that Christ will then have power over all men whereby he can reward the righteous and torment the wicked? When did he not possess this power? When were not all things in subjection to Christ enough for these purposes? The subjection of all things to Christ must mean something, and it is reasonable to believe that it means the reconciliation of the heart to holiness. Can a soul in sin, employed in blaspheming the Incommunicable Name, be said to be in subjection to Christ in any way that answers to the text? I do not think any will contend for it.

The only subjection which is acceptable to Christ is a broken and contrite heart, which he will not despise. The plan, then, of the Gospel is universal submission to Christ in holiness and happiness.

The delivery of the kingdom of Christ to the Father is declared in the last clause of the passage quoted, of which I have before taken notice in this work in order to show the dependence of Christ on the Eternal and Self-existent. Then, it is said, "God shall be all in all." (1 Cor. xv. 28.) In what sense will God be all in all at the close of the Redeemer's process that he is not now, or always was? Answer: he that dwelleth in love, dwelleth in God, and God in him. When all men are brought to love God supremely, and their fellow-creatures as themselves, it will then be manifest that we are nothing only as we exist in God; therefore, God will be all. And as the eternal spirit of love, which is the governing principle of the heavenly man, will be the governing principle of each soul thus reconciled to the law of love, it my be justly said that God is in all. See 1 Cor. xv. 47-49:

> The first man is of the earth, earthy; the second man is the Lord from heaven. As is the earthy, such are they also that are earthy; and as is the heavenly, such are they also that are heavenly. And as we have borne the image of the earthy, we shall also bear the image of the heavenly.

As we have all been partakers of the earthy Adam, so, the apostle argues, we shall be partakers in the resurrection of the Second Adam, whom he calls the Lord from heaven. See verses 51-54:

> Behold, I will show you a mystery; we shall not all sleep, but we shall all be changed, in a moment, in the twinkling of an eye, at the last trump; for the trumpet shall sound, and the dead shall be raised incorruptible, and we shall be changed. For this corruptible shall put on incorruption, and this mortal must put on immortality. So when this corruptible shall have put on incorruption, and this mortal shall have put on immortality, then shall be brought to pass the saying that is written, death is swallowed up in victory.

If death, sin, and sorrow are to remain as long as God exists, how can it be said death is swallowed up in victory? If the apostle believed any part of the family of man would finally be excluded from the blessings of the Gospel, why did he not just hint something of it in this account of the close of the mediatorial kingdom? Did he consider it a matter of too small a moment to mention? If he did, he is inexcusable for precluding the idea by plain and positive testimony. See his conclusion (1. Cor. xv. 55):

> O death! where is thy sting? O grave! where is thy victory? The sting of death is sin; and the strength of sin is the law. But thanks be to God, who giveth us the victory through our Lord Jesus Christ.

If sin remain without end, it being the sting of death, when the question is asked, "O death, where is thy sting?" sin may answer, "Here I am and here I will be in spite of him who undertook to destroy the works of the devil, and here I will boast of my power as long as he does of his, whom angels adore, and I hate!" See Phil. iii. 21:

Who shall change our vile body, that it may be fashioned like unto his glorious body, according to the working whereby he is able even to subdue all things unto himself.

Observe, who shall change our vile body. In a former quotation it is said, "we shall all be changed"; and in the present passage it is said, "whereby he is able even to subdue all things unto himself." In a former quotation it is said, "And when all things shall be subdued unto him."

Let us hear what our blessed Lord himself says in respect to his mission. St. John v. 22-23:

For the Father judgeth no man; but hath committed all judgment unto the Son; that all men should honor the Son, even as they honor the Father. He that honoreth not the Son honoreth not the Father which hath sent him.

In the sense in which this passage was spoken, it is evident that the sinner does neither honor the Father nor the Son, and the plain testimony of the text is that all men should honor both.

Compare this with Phil. ii. 9-11:

Wherefore God also hath highly exalted him, and given him a name which is above every name; that at the name of Jesus every knee should bow, of things in heaven, and things in earth, and things under the earth; and that every tongue should confess that Jesus Christ is Lord, to the glory of God the Father.

As in the other passage the exaltation of the Savior is first spoken of, and then the grand intention in his exaltation shown; so in this; there it is for the purpose that all men should honor him; and here it is that unto him every knee should bow, of things in heaven, and things in the earth, and things under the earth; and that every tongue should confess that Jesus Christ is Lord, to the glory of God the Father.

Of this glorious and soul-reviving truth the prophet Isaiah was not ignorant, but speaks of it most clearly. See chap. xlv. 22-25:

Look unto me and be ye saved all the ends of the earth; for I am God, and there is none else. I have sworn by myself, the word is gone out of my mouth in righteousness, and shall not return, that unto me every knee shall bow, every tongue shall swear. Surely, shall say, in the Lord have I righteousness and strength: even to him shall come; and all that are incensed against him shall be ashamed. In the Lord shall all the seen of Israel be justified, and shall glory.

The reader will observe I have left out some supplied words in the above quotation, by which the passage reads without ambiguity.

Had the inspired prophet been possessed of an accurate knowledge of the dispute in which I am engaged, I do not see how he could have written a sentence more pertinently to my argument; and I have not a doubt but the Spirit intended the passage for the same purpose for which I have used it.

St. Paul, in the eighth chapter of Romans, shows the extent of redemption in so strong terms as to admit of no possible evasion. See Rom. v. 22-23:

For we know that the whole creation groaneth and travaileth in pain together until now. And not only they, but ourselves also, which have the first fruits of the Spirit, even we ourselves groan within ourselves, waiting for the adoption, to wit, the redemption of our body.

If the reader will be at the trouble of examining this passage with its connection, that for which I contend will appear plainly proved by it.

There is no end to proofs of universal reconciliation to God; for everything of a moral nature testifies to it, and all material nature is a figure of it. The ministry of reconciliation, which, St. Paul says, was committed to himself and others, is that God was in Christ reconciling the world unto himself, not imputing unto them their trespasses. The truth of Christ's dying for all is the foundation of the apostle's argument on this subject; which truth, the apostle says, he was constrained to believe by the love of Christ; for thus saith he (2 Cor. v. 14-15):

The love of Christ constraineth us; because we thus judge, that if one died for all, then were all dead; and that he died for all, that they which live should not henceforth live unto themselves, but unto him which died for them, and rose again.

I may as well stop here as anywhere, for as I just said, there is no end; and if those Scriptures which I have quoted be true, that which I have endeavored to prove is proved; but if they be not, more of the same testimony would prove nothing.

There is but one method left for my opponent by which he can further oppose me; and that is, by denying the whole system of divine revelation and man's susceptibility of rational ideas. But as that would equally destroy all for which he would contend, he will undoubtedly be cautious.

We now see clearly that it is God's will, according to his eternal purpose, purposed in himself, that all men should finally be *holy* and *happy*; that it was the intention of the Savior's mission; that the prophets, by the spirit of prophecy, long foresaw this universal and godlike glorious plan of grace; that every good principle in man stands up in testimony of so divine a system; that the happiness of all moral beings is wrapped up in the glorious issue of the ministration of reconciliation; and that it is, in reality, opposed by none but by unreconciled being, unholy principles, and unlawful desires.

And shall we say that the eternal good will of him who dwelt in the bush must fail at last? Must the testimony of the prophets fall to the ground? Must the captain of our salvation, who warred in righteousness, who reddened his garments in his own blood, who bore the sins of the world, and suffered death in agony, to obtain his lawful inheritance, be robbed of them at last? Were this believed in heaven the royal diadem would fall from the head of him whom all the heaven adores, and the highest archangel would faint away! But, blessed be the Lord, and blessed be his truth, its divine power shall cause the Leviathan of infidelity to bite the ground, shall rend the veil which is cast over all nations, and shall more and more manifest divine righteousness and the name in which it is found, in which name alone is salvation.

In the days of the apostles, the greatest object in preaching the Gospel of Christ was to prove him to be the Savior of the world, the true Messiah of the law, urging that he died for all, that he made no distinction between Jew and Gentile, but had broken down the partition-wall between them, for the glorious purpose of making of the twain one new man in everlasting fellowship and eternal peace. But how hath the gold changed, how hath the most fine gold become dim? The main apparent object, at the present day, is to prove the object of the Savior's mission, as it respects the salvation of sinners, extremely limited; and that but few of the human race will finally be the redeemed of the Lord to the praise of his glory; that the great adversary of righteousness will obtain a much larger conquest of souls than Christ himself; and, oh shocking to name, eternal justice is profaned by being called to assist the serpent's designs in the endless duration of sin and rebellion against God!

Those whom the Lord hath blessed with a belief of universal holiness and happiness are proscribed as heretics, infidels, offscourings of the earth, friends to nothing but sin, and enemies to nothing but God and holiness; opening a door to licentiousness of every abominable species, destroyers of the pure religion of Christ, and nuisances to society. But is it, in reality, manifesting a love to sin to argue its total destruction by the power of divine righteousness? Is it manifesting enmity against God and the religion of Jesus to contend for the propriety of all men's serving him in holiness and happiness? And are we nuisances to society because we endeavor to persuade all men to love God and one another? Can these things be displeasing to him who was born in Bethlehem? Will he not rather greatly bless such labors, though performed by those as little esteemed in the world as the poor fishermen who left their nets and followed the despised Nazarene?

Let us ask a few questions. Which reflects the most honor on the divine character, to contend it was necessary for him to create millions of rational creatures to hate him and every divine communication he makes to them to all eternity, to live in endless rebellion against him, and endure inconceivable torments as long as God exists, or to suppose him able and willing to make all his rational creatures love and adore him, yield obedience to his divine law, and exist in union and happiness with himself?

Which reflects most honor on the Savior, to say that but few will obtain salvation by him, and though he died for all men, yet his death will benefit but few, or to say with the prophet, "He shall see of the travail of the soul and be satisfied, having reconciled all things to God, through the peace made by the blood of the cross"?*

If there be joy in heaven over one sinner that repenteth, more than over ninety and nine just persons who need no repentance, which would yield the most joy to the heavenly hosts, the repentance of one-fourth of mankind or the whole? If the servants of Christ here on earth desire the increase of holiness and the decrease of sin, which would be most agreeable to such a desire, the belief that the greatest part of mankind will grow more and more sinful to all eternity, or to believe that sin will continually decrease, and righteousness increase, until the former is wholly destroyed and the latter becomes *universal?*

To answer the above questions, so as to favor my opponent's argument, is more than any one would be willing to do; and which, if done, would involve an endless train of ideas too glaringly absurd to be supported. But to answer them agreeably to the nature of divine truth opens to infinite beauties more serene than

---

* Ballou combined two Bible passages here:— Isa. liii. 11 reads: "He shall see of the travail of his soul, and shall be satisfied: by his knowledge shall my righteous servant justify many; for he shall bear their iniquities." —and Col. i. 19-20 reads: "For it pleased the Father that in him should all fullness dwell; and, having made peace through the blood of his cross, by him to reconcile all things unto himself..." —Editor.

the morning, and more glorious than the noon day. God the fountain of living waters and the essence of eternal life, is seen by faith in Jesus the same to all rational beings, the author, supporter, and blesser of them. Christ Jesus, the head of every man, is beheld as the brightness of the Father's glory, and express image of his person through whom the Eternal hath manifested the riches of his grace, the eternal councils of his love to the world, brought life and immortality to light, and manifested our eternal sonship in the Second Adam.

Each holy desire, as the fruit of the Spirit, in the souls of those who believe, feasts on the rich promises of Abraham's God, believing him faithful who hath promised. Heaven hath already received the heave offering of the first ripe fruits, and the fields are white, ready to harvest. O ye laborers in the vineyard of the Lord, be ye not idle. What an extensive field is here in which for the mind to expand and send its desires abroad! The transcendent beauties of salvation have visited the dark regions of mortality, as light and heat from the vernal sun visit the cold and dark north, turning frozen lands into fruitful fields, taking the icy fetters from limpid streams which bend their course to the fountain, bringing the time of the singing of birds, and causing the voice of the turtle to be heard.

"I am come," says Jesus, "to send a fire on the earth; and what will I, if it be already kindled?" (Luke xii. 49.) All the passages, which allude to a dispensation of fire, which we have observed, in this work, are direct evidences, to prove the destruction of sin and all sinful works, the purification of sinners, and their eternal reconciliation to holiness and happiness. This fire will either overcome sin, or be overcome by it. But who will argue the latter? If none, then let the former be acknowledged.

If you say, these things appear differently from what you expected they would before your inquiry; and you find something more interesting than tradition has taught you; if you feel soft, in your mind, towards the so much despised doctrine of universal holiness and happiness; if you can believe heaven large enough to contain mankind, and begin to breathe in the air of unbounded benevolence, and feel faith mingled with your desires for the destruction of sin, and the increase of holiness, then come still further. The knowledge of these things is progressive, and obtained only by degrees. Let us still go on and view the heavenly beauties yet to be unfolded in the plan of the Gospel.

We well know there are many difficulties to be surmounted; to profess universal salvation will subject some to excommunication from regular churches; others to the pain of being neglected by their neighbors; others to be violently opposed by their companions; and, in many instances, undoubtedly the father will be against the son, and the son against the father; the mother against the daughter, and the daughter against the mother; and a man's enemies may be those of his own house. But can such difficulties excuse us for not owning him who, for us, bore the cross and despised the shame?

All denominations, since the world began, have experienced some difficulties in their first establishment. Christ and his apostles wrestled hard, and encountered great opposition, even to the loss of all earthly things, with life itself. Since the apostasy, the denominations which arose out of Popery have, in thousands of instances, suffered more than duty calls us to suffer in a land of liberty and toleration.

But some will say, there are none who profess the doctrine in my vicinity except some of the lower class of people; and if I rank myself with them, my titles of honor will do me no good, and my road to the temple of fame will be forever intercepted. One will say I must believe the doctrine, I cannot argue against it, but I will say nothing about it, lest I should be mistrusted; I would gladly embrace the opportunity which Nicodemus did, who went to Jesus by night; but to come out boldly, to the knowledge of the world, is too great a sacrifice. Says another, I am convinced of the truth of the doctrine, but I have preached so much against it, have warned my hearers so much to shun that heresy, I am now ashamed to tell them I believe it. Another feels so dependent on his neighbors, he wishes to have them go forward first. All these circumstances, and many more, bear great weight with various persons, in various circumstances, causing great labor of mind; and those who are under such influences may be said to be heavy laden. We know of no better remedy for those cases, than an attention to the exhortation of Christ, who said (Matt. xi. 28-30):

> Come unto me all ye that labor and are heavy laden, and I will give you rest; take my yoke upon you and learn of me; for I am meek and lowly in heart; and you shall find rest unto your souls; for my yoke is easy and my burden is light.

The reader may judge, from those circumstances, whether this doctrine be pleasing to the carnal mind, as its enemies say. Was it pleasing to the Pharisees of old to be taught by Christ and his disciples that publicans and harlots should enter the kingdom of heaven before them? Yes, just as pleasing to their carnal minds, as it is to a professed preacher of Christ who can thank God that he is better than other men, to tell him that those upon whom he looks as much viler than himself stand in no more need of pardon than he does.

St. Paul, before his conversion to Christianity, undoubtedly looked on the doctrine of Christ to be exactly calculated to please wicked men, as the most part of those who were discipled by it were publicans and sinners; and he well knew, that the foundation of their hope was the forgiveness of sin. This he despised, as did many of his equals in the Jewish religion; feeling themselves whole, they felt no need of a physician. They supposed the Gospel to be a doctrine every way calculated to vitiate and immoralize mankind. Undoubtedly the Pharisees often said of the disciples of Christ, their religion is perfectly suited to their characters; they are sinners, and know not the law; and they have contrived a very easy way to get to heaven.

But if we ask St. Paul, after his conversion, what he thought of these things, he would undoubtedly give a very different account. For when the Lord met him in the way and gave him to understand his real character, and what he was doing, he was astonished and fell to the earth; his sins were set in order before him, and his soul was greatly troubled. In this situation, he learned the necessity of the doctrine which he had despised; experienced the necessity of its pardoning mercy; and became as willing to endure persecution, for its sake, as he had been to persecute it before.

When it is understood that Gospel salvation is salvation from carnal mindedness and all its relative ills, to a reconciliation to the law of the spirit of life in Christ Jesus; if all men were thus saved, it would not be argued that it is pleasing to the carnal mind. As the doctrine for which we contend is entirely the reverse of carnal mindedness, so it is equally opposed to licentiousness; for what can be a stronger restraint on the passions than a belief in God's universal goodness, and that all men are the objects of his mercy? Such a belief, when it has its proper effects in the mind, raises a supreme affection for God, and kindles the sacred fire of love and unbounded benevolence to mankind. If any would dispute me on my statement of the consequences of this faith, I have greatly the advantage; as my opponent does not possess this faith, he cannot tell the effects of it so well as one can who does. However, I will not make use of that advantage, having argument in my power that is more than sufficient. Let my adversary state his argument, that we may see the strength of it.

The fact is, he has no argument; he can only assert, "the doctrine is not productive of love to God or man, but the reverse; and if he believed it, he would commit every sin that was in his power." Is it hard to see, that my opponent has made a very fair and full profession of his love to sin, in place of his love to God; and a strong desire to injure his fellow men, in room of serving them in love? What was the elder brother angry for? At what did he grumble? And why did he refuse to go into his father's house? Because the father had received the prodigal, and treated him kindly. (Luke xv. 11-32.) At what did the laborers grumble who bore the burden and heat of the day? Because those who had wrought but one hour received as much as they, and received their money first. (Matt. xx. 1-16.) At what did the Pharisees and scribes murmur, when they saw all the publicans and sinners come to Jesus to hear him? Because he did not condemn them to hopeless despair, but kindly received them. (Luke v. 30, etc.) At what do our opposers rage? At what are they dissatisfied? Not because we exclude them from any privilege, or blessing of the Gospel. What then? We are sorry to name it. It is because we extend those blessings further, and hope they will do more good than what suits them!

As the doctrine of universal holiness and happiness opens an infinite field in which for the mind to expatiate, and learn the goodness of God in all his works and providence, it is the most animating to a benevolent soul of any that was ever believed in our world, and lays the broadest foundation for exhortation to deny ungodliness and worldly lusts, to live sober, righteous and godly lives. How strong are the inducements, from such glorious views of God and his mercy, to lead us to imitate such unbounded goodness in all our intentions and actions. And being fully convinced that our happiness is in union with our duty, those who fully believe in the consequences of atonement, as we have argued them, will see the propriety of our endeavoring to stir up their pure minds by way of remembrance, exhorting them to good works in all faithfulness in whatever situation duty may call them, or whatever the part may be which our heavenly Father hath called them to act, in his divine and delightsome service. The duty enjoined on the believer of this doctrine is as much more extensive than the duty enjoined by any other faith, as the faith itself is more extensive; and its delights are so, likewise.

If a poor man was offered a thousand pounds for a day's labor, it would undoubtedly be a very strong inducement to him to labor. But it is to be observed, in this case, that it is not the labor itself which is the object, but the large sum of money with which the laborer expects to be rewarded. It is not the labor in which the man delights; could he obtain his money, without the work, it would be his choice. But when the labor itself is all the enjoyment, and the whole object is obedience, the laborer will not wish the time short, or the duty small; no, eternity is none too long for the soul to contemplate laboring in the endless delights of obedience to his God.

Those who believe a future state of happiness depends on certain duties performed by them, undoubtedly intend to do those duties sometime before they die; and it is often said that a procrastination of those duties, on which so much depends, is dangerous as life is uncertain; yet they had rather let it alone until old age deprives them of the common comforts of life; at which time, they may about as well be employed in the dull and disagreeable task of being good as any thing else. But those who consider their duty as their meat and drink ought not to need much inviting to feed on dainties so rich. We should hardly believe a man to be in his right mind, who, for eating a good meal of victuals, should charge the price of it. "In keeping thy commandments, there is great reward." (Psalm xix. 11.)

By these observations, the reader will see how needful it is for us, at all times, to attend to our duty, because "now is the accepted time, and now is the day of salvation" (2 Cor. vi. 2); to every willing and obedient soul who feels the power of atoning grace, salvation is present. Truly it is said of wisdom (Prov. ix. 1-2):

> She hath builded her house, she hath hewn out her seven pillars: she hath killed her beasts; she hath mingled her wine; she hath also furnished her table.

God, in infinite wisdom, has constituted all moral beings so that their duty is their happiness, and strict obedience fullness of joy.

Why, then, my brethren, shall we starve? Why live poor? Why should we be so parsimonious of those heavenly stores that can never be exhausted? (Matt. v. 6.)

> Blessed are they who hunger and thirst after righteousness for they shall be filled.

(Luke xi. 9.)

> Ask, and ye shall receive; seek and ye shall find; knock, and it shall be opened unto you.

God forbids none (Rev. xx. 17):

> The Spirit and the bride say, come; and let him that heareth, say, come.... And whoever will, let him take of the fountain of the water of life freely.

Remember the salvation which God wills is a salvation from sin. Then, as much as you desire salvation, you will wish to avoid sin and wickedness. There are none who would say they did not want salvation; but how many are there who say, they want it by their own conduct! No man, understandingly, wants salvation any further than he wants more holiness.

The Universalist, who is really so, prizes his duty as his heaven, as his peace, and his most sublime enjoyment. How then shall we be so lost, so blind, and so deceived, as to wish to shun our duty and our happiness? If we really believe those things, and desire that others may be brought to see and believe the same, let us endeavor, in the first place, to prove to all men that such a belief is of real service in cultivating our morals and in regulating our behavior. And, secondly, by using our abilities as God hath given, in cool dispassionate reasoning, with those who do not believe; contending for nothing but the pure principles of love, in meekness and all gentleness. Never argue for the sake of *will* nor for mastery; and, shunning every appearance of sophistry, never suffer yourselves to be anxious about the issue of conversation; but speak the words of truth and soberness, and leave the event to be directed by the spirit of God. Falsehood is so apt to detect itself, that an argument is generally best conducted when the disputant is refuted by consequences arising from his own statements; and if he cannot see and understand them for himself, it will do no good to see them for him. If we can see for ourselves, we do well.

If the Lord of the harvest hath graciously been pleased to call you by his grace to preach the word of his Gospel to his purchased possession; to sound abroad the trumpet of salvation, and to feed the sheep and lambs of the one true shepherd; then remember that it is required of stewards that they are found faithful. St. Paul declared himself a debtor both to the Greeks and Barbarians, to the wise and the unwise. He having received a dispensation of the Gospel, the grace of which belonged to all men, he thereby became a debtor to all. And if we have received a dispensation of the same Gospel, we are debtors to all whom this Gospel concerns.

How happy is a friend who has good news to communicate to his companions; and surely it is an office much to be desired to carry good news to the distressed. See the officer when he reads a pardon to one who expects immediate death: his soul bursts through his eyes in streams of joy, while he pronounces the words which give life to the dead. But how much more excellent are the labors of those whose feet are beautiful on the mountains, who publish peace in the Redeemer's name, even glad tidings unto all people.

Much watchfulness is necessary, lest the law of the carnal or old man gets the government of the mind. I will venture to say there never was a preacher more ready, on all occasions, than the old man which we are exhorted to put off; he is willing at all times to assist, never waiting to be called. He has no objections to preaching about Christ, if Christ be not preached. He is perfectly willing to say that salvation is all of God, and that Christ is a whole Savior; but then it is indispensably necessary that he should do something; such as asking, seeking, knocking; or if it be only accepting of offered mercy is all he wants. It may be the reader will wonder a little at what I here say, as I have just quoted the exhortation, to ask, to seek, to knock, etc.; but I wish to be understood, that we must ask, seek, and knock, not in the name or nature of the earthly Adam, but in the name and nature of the heavenly man.

The old serpent, the devil, is never better pleased than when he can do something which he thinks lays God under some obligation to him. If the carnal or old man get so baffled as to be reduced to give up his influence respecting our eternal life in Jesus, he will immediately propose, in his struggles, that all he can do is to ensure a blessed state for some considerable time after we die, say for a thousand years, or any given time; then all must depend on the Savior. If the earthly Adam can get us up Jacob's ladder a few steps, he is willing that Christ should do something by and by.

Now the object of all those devices, of which we are not ignorant (as St. Paul says), is to keep us in the service of the flesh; but remember, he that soweth to the flesh, shall of the flesh reap corruption. A Pharisee, who feels as if something was coming to him more than others receive, perhaps will not be scrupulous about the exact quantity. He only wishes to have proper attention paid him; if he can flatter himself with a higher seat in heaven than those are to have, on whom he looks as worse than himself, it satisfies his carnal pride. Perhaps a period of punishment for sinners after death, in which they may be justly corrected for not being so good and holy as this Pharisee, would give him much satisfaction. He would then be willing to have the poor wretches delivered from absolute misery, and enjoy some small conveniences.

O, how hard it is, to be a humble disciple of the meek and lowly Jesus. It is death to carnal mind. If I preach the Gospel all my life long, spend all my time and strength for the good of mankind, and the honor of my Savior, shall I not have something more hereafter than one who has mocked and derided me? Answer if I have, in truth and meekness, preached Christ, and have been faithful in his cause, ought I not to be thankful that he has enabled me so to do? Have I been the loser, unless we are paid in the world to come by having some privilege granted us which another may not enjoy? O, blush, my soul, if thy follies rise so high.

No, every moment's faithfulness has been supplied with streams of divine consolation; and it ought to be remembered, that the preacher never refreshes others, unless he himself is refreshed. If I have professed to preach Christ, but have preached myself in place of him, undoubtedly I may think there is something coming, as my living has been very poor while I have thus labored; but the truth is, our reward has been equal to our service.

I am willing to acknowledge that carnal mind often contends, that I have done so well, I ought in consequence to expect high approbations; and I begin to look down on those whom we fancy of less magnitude. But, O, the viperous sting! Well might an apostle say (Rom. vii. 23),

> I find a law in my members warring against the law of my mind, bringing me into captivity to the law of sin which is in my members.

Says the same apostle (Eph. iii. 8),

> Unto me, who am less than the least of all saints, is this grace given, that I should preach among the Gentiles the unsearchable riches of Christ.

Upon what high advantages did he calculate, above those who were much less in labor than himself?

But, says the reader, will not St. Paul fare better than the worst of sinners in eternity? Judge from what he says (1 Tim. i. 15):

> This is a faithful saying, and worthy of all acceptation, that Christ Jesus came into the world to save sinners, of whom I am chief.

The more humble we are, the greater our enjoyments. But when all are completely humbled, and perfectly reconciled; when all old things are done away, and all things become new; when he, who sitteth upon the throne, maketh all things new in deed and in truth, we believe all strife, concerning who shall be great in the kingdom of heaven, will be at an end.

Ye, who preach righteousness in the great congregations of the people, forget not the exhortation of the Captain of our salvation: "Learn of me." (Matt. xi. 29.) What good will all our labors do unless we learn of Christ? If we learn of him, he will be unto us, wisdom, righteousness, sanctification and redemption; and we shall preach, not ourselves, but Christ Jesus our Lord, and ourselves the servants of the people, for Jesus' sake.

Remember, again, the exhortation of him who is the leader and commander of the people, "Search the scriptures." (John v. 39.) Make yourselves acquainted with, and have free recourse to, this great store-house of divine riches, that you may be ready to "deal a portion to seven and also to eight." "Ye are the salt of the earth." (Matt. v. 13.) As salt preserves and seasons meats, so that they are acceptable, so ought the ministers of righteousness to endeavor, as far as possible, to preserve mankind from sin, that they may be acceptable members of the church of Christ. Verse 13 continued:

> But if the salt have lost its savor, wherewith shall it be salted? it is thenceforth good for nothing, but to be cast out and trodden under foot of men.

We cannot be profitable to others, unless we have the savor of the Spirit within us; this lost, and we are good for nothing; and in room of having a mouth, and wisdom, to put gainsayers to silence, we shall be overcome by them, and they will tread us under their feet (Jude i. 3):

> Contend earnestly for the faith once delivered to the saints.

But be sure to remember that (2 Cor. x. 4):

> The weapons of our warfare are not carnal, but spiritual, and mighty through God.

Carnal mind frequently urges the necessity of contending

earnestly for the faith once delivered to the saints; but then we must contend in a coat of mail, and with the weapons of him who sought the life of the Son of Jesse. Be prepared to meet every kind of opposition; we must be attacked on every side, the adversary will not leave one stone unturned, nor a weapon in his armor untried. Be cautious of any system of divinity; remember (Prov. iv. 18):

> The path of the just is a shining light, which shineth more and more unto the perfect day.

The moment we fancy ourselves infallible, every one must come to our peculiarities or we cast them away. Even the truth may be held in unrighteousness. Daniel's God was undoubtedly the true God; but we do not conceive Darius any more the real friend of that God, when he made a decree that all people should worship him, than he was when he made the decree that no petition should be asked of any God or man for thirty days save of himself.

The cause of truth wants nothing in its service but the fruits of the Spirit, which are love, joy, peace, gentleness, goodness, faith, meekness, and temperance. All the divisions and subdivisions which now exist among Christians, or ever have existed, were caused wholly by the want of those graces. Should we be tenacious about certain sentiments and peculiarities of faith, the time is not far distant when Universalists, who have suffered every kind of contemptuous treatment from the enemies of the doctrine, will be at war among themselves and be trodden under foot of the gentiles. Having begun in the Spirit, do not think to be made perfect by the flesh. In order to imitate our Savior, let us, like him, have compassion on the ignorant and those whom we view to be out of the way. Attend to the exhortation (Heb. xiii. 1):

> Let brotherly love continue.

If we agree in brotherly love, there is no disagreement that can do us any injury; but if we do not, no other agreement can do us any good. Let us keep a strict guard against the enemy "that sows discord among brethren." (Prov. vi. 19.) Let us endeavor to "keep the unity of the Spirit in the bonds of peace." (Eph. iv. 3.) May charity, that heaven born companion of the human heart, never forsake us; and may the promise of the Savior be fulfilled concerning us (Matt. xxviii. 20):

Lo I am with you even unto the end of the world.

You have now, kind reader, cast your eye over these pages; perhaps you feel to say, "the doctrine of universal holiness and happiness cannot be true, notwithstanding all the author has said in favor of it"; and if so, I condemn you not. The time has been when I believed as little of the doctrine as you now do; I never adopted the belief of universal holiness and happiness out of choice, but from the force of real or supposed evidence. And I know you cannot believe it on any other ground.

I hope, however, you feel no enmity to so glorious a system of God's grace; I hope you have the spirit of Christ, and wish well to mankind. I have, besure, great consolation in believing that our Redeemer has many faithful servants and loving disciples in the world who do not believe in the extensiveness of salvation as I do, and I often take great satisfaction in feasts of charity with such brethren. St. Peter was undoubtedly a lover of Christ and his Gospel before he was taught by the sea of Joppa to call no man common or unclean. The rest of the disciples, who were dissatisfied with his preaching the Gospel to the uncircumcised, were doubtless possessed of the spirit of Christ, which caused them to glorify God when they had more extensive views of the Gospel through Peter's communications.

As far as I see men walk in the spirit of love to God and one another, I feel an union with them, whether their particular sentiments are mine or not. Men cannot believe at will; we believe as evidence appears to our mind. The times have been when each denomination has been proscribed, and, in some measure, persecuted. Each as it rose has been censured by those who could not fall in with their doctrine; and what does all this condemning one another prove? —only the imperfections of all, and the badness of the human heart.

You will not think evil of me, kind reader, if I exhort you not to feel too hard against what you may find to be your duty to acknowledge. It grieved Peter when his Lord asked him the third time if he loved him, as he had denied him thrice. There are many Universalists now who have frequent occasion to confess how hard they have been against the doctrine, and how much they have spoken unadvisedly with their lips against what they now rejoice to believe is truth, and humbly adore the Savior of sinners for opening their eyes to behold such unspeakable beauties. If you attend to the exhortation to grow in grace and in the knowledge of our Lord Jesus Christ, undoubtedly you may see more of the riches of his goodness than you now do.

The prophet Ezekiel's knowledge of the holy waters was progressive, and obtained by degrees. When he was first led into the waters, they were only to his ankles; but he went still further, and they were to his knees; he went still further, and they were to his loins; he went further, and the waters were risen, waters for men to swim in, a river that no man could pass. Had the prophet refused to travel in these waters after he first entered them, he would not have known nor believed them to be so multitudinous as they were. A soul in the earliest moments of heavenly love is first unspeakably charmed with the untold beauties and graces of his Redeemer; next, wife, children, father, mother, brothers, sisters, all friends; directly enemies; and finally all mankind, are embraced in the extended arms of heavenly love and divine benevolence.

I close this work, humbly hoping and expecting the glorious increase and extensive growth of what I have (though feebly) contended for, viz. the holiness and happiness of mankind. I look with strong expectation for that period when all sin and every degree of unreconciliation will be destroyed by the divine power of that love which is stronger than death, which many waters cannot quench, nor the floods drown; in which alone I put my trust, and in which my hope is anchored for all mankind; earnestly praying, that the desire of the righteous may not be cut off.

The fullness of times will come, and the times of the restitution of all things will be accomplished. Then shall truth be victorious, and all error flee to eternal night. Then shall universal songs of honor be sung to the praise of him who liveth forever and ever. All death, sorrow, and crying shall be done away; pains and disorders shall be no more felt, temptations no more trouble the lovers of God, nor sin poison the human heart. The blessed hand of the once crucified shall wipe tears from off all faces. O, transporting thought! Then shall the blessed Savior see of the travail of his soul, and be satisfied, when, through his mediation, universal nature shall be brought in perfect union with truth and holiness, and the spirit of God fill all rational beings. Then shall the law of the spirit of life in Christ Jesus, which maketh free from the law of sin, become the governing principle of the whole man once made subject to vanity, once enthralled in darkness, sin and misery, but then, delivered from the bondage of corruption, and restored to perfect reconciliation to God in the heavenly Adam.

Then shall the great object of the Savior's mission be accomplished. Then shall the question be asked, O death where is thy sting? But death shall not be, to give the answer. And, O grave, where is thy victory? But the boaster shall be silent. The Son shall deliver up the kingdom to God the Father; the eternal radiance shall smile, and GOD shall be ALL in ALL.

❖ THE END ❖

APPENDIX

Biography of Hosea Ballou (1851)

The following biography of Hosea Ballou was written by Thomas Whittemore, as a preface to Ballou's "Valedictory Discourse," published in January, 1851, by James M. Usher of Boston, as the first in a series of Universalist sermons; this series was later collected in book form under the title *The Universalist Pulpit*. At the time Whittemore wrote this brief biography, Ballou was still alive, and still preaching. Whittemore went on to publish a four volume biography of Ballou, completed in 1855.

Rev. Hosea Ballou, Senior Pastor of the Second Universalist Society in Boston, will enter his eighty-first year in April next. His father was Rev. Maturin Ballou. The latter was born in Rhode Island, where a large part of his life was spent. He officiated there, for some years, as a Baptist clergyman; and, about 1767 or 1768, he removed to Richmond, N. H., then a new settlement, where the subject of this sketch was born, on the 30th of April, 1771.

Hosea Ballou spent the chief part of his minority with his father. The doctrine of Universalism had been embraced by a few individuals in that vicinity, but was regarded by the people generally, especially church members, with great abhorrence. Young Ballou, in his nineteenth year, joined the Baptist church, of which his father had been pastor. It was, however, but a short time afterward that he became doubtful of the truth of the doctrine of endless misery; and these doubts increased, until he was fully convinced of its falsity, and of the truth of the great and glorious doctrine of the final holiness and happiness of all men. He was excommunicated for this belief, although his character, in the view of the church, was blameless. He soon began to proclaim his new opinions, and preached his first sermon in the town in which he was born, in the fall of 1791, from 1 Cor. i. 30. Immediately after, he commenced to travel in different parts of the country, preaching and teaching school; and we may name the County of Worcester, in Massachusetts, and the States of Rhode Island and Connecticut, as the principal scenes of his labors.

The place in which he was first settled, as a preacher, was Dana,

Mass. In 1796, he was married to Miss Ruth Washburn, of Williamsburg, Mass.; a lady who is still living, and who has done all to make his life a happy one that it is in the power of woman to do. While Mr. Ballou resided in Dana, he preached principally in that town, and in Oxford and Charlton. In 1799 he attended the General Convention of Universalists in Woodstock, Vermont, which was the first occasion of his going into the interior of that State. This visit made him acquainted with several of the prominent Universalists of that region; and, in consequence of this acquaintance, he removed, in 1803, to Barnard, and took charge of the societies in Barnard, Woodstock, Hartland, Bethel, and Bridgewater. He resided in the first named of these towns.

Soon after his settlement, he wrote his *Notes on the Parables*, the first edition of which was published in 1804, in pamphlet form. It was greatly enlarged in the second edition, which was published in Portsmouth, N. H., in 1812. Soon after the *Notes* were published, Mr. Ballou proceeded to write his *Treatise on Atonement*, in which he took the ground that God was never unreconciled to man; that man was the party who needed reconciliation, for God is love, from eternity to eternity; and that God's love to sinners was the cause of Christ being sent, by the Father, to redeem them. He held that Christ was not God himself, but the Son of God,— a distinct being from the Father,— a created being;— a doctrine which he had believed and preached for ten years before the *Treatise* was published in 1805. He must, therefore, be regarded as the earliest American defender of Unitarianism the country has produced.

In 1809, Mr. Ballou removed to Portsmouth, N. H., where he was installed November 8th, the sermon on the occasion being preached by Rev. Edward Turner, then of Salem. While residing here, he had several controversies with the clergymen of the place, among whom may be named Rev. Messrs. Walton and Buckminster. Mr. Ballou remained in Portsmouth until June, 1815, when he accepted the invitation of the Universalist Society in Salem, Mass., to become their pastor.

His connection with the Society in Salem was not of long continuance, for he removed to Boston, and became the pastor of the Second Universalist Society in that town, in December, 1817. This Society had just finished their house of worship on School Street. They never for a moment had a thought of seeking any other pastor than the Rev. Hosea Ballou, if it were possible to obtain his services; and, accordingly, two months before the house was ready for dedication, a letter of inquiry was despatched to him, to draw out his sentiments in regard to a removal to

Boston. In the mean time the house was hurried on to completion. Rev. Messrs. Jones, of Gloucester, Turner, of Charlestown, Ballou of Salem, and Dean of Boston, were invited to join in the dedicatory services; Mr. Jones to preach the sermon, and the others to arrange the remaining services at their discretion. The dedication took place on Wednesday, October 16th; and, on the following Tuesday, a meeting of the proprietors was held, and Mr. Ballou was invited to take the pastoral charge by a unanimous vote. The salary was fixed, at first, at thirteen hundred dollars per annum, to which donations of fuel were occasionally made. Mr. Ballou was installed on December 25, 1817. Rev. Paul Dean preached, on the occasion, from Acts xx. 24. He also gave the fellowship of the churches. Rev. E. Turner, of Charlestown, made the installing prayer, and gave the charge. Rev. Joshua Flagg, who had succeeded Mr. Ballou at Salem, offered the concluding prayer.

Thus was Mr. Ballou duly installed as pastor of Second Universalist Society in Boston. The congregations that attended on his ministry were exceedingly large. He soon became widely known for his eloquence and boldness, and the novel nature of the subjects discussed by him. His preaching was of a controversial and doctrinal character. He explained, in his discourses, those texts which had been supposed to teach the doctrine of a judgment in the future state, and endless torment. He was repeatedly called on, by letter, from inquirers after truth, to preach from particular texts of this character; and, as he gave public notice of the times when he would consider such passages, his audiences were immensely large. It was usual to see the meeting-house filled, in the forenoon, so that it was difficult to obtain a seat; in the afternoon, many would be obliged to stand, especially in the galleries, and around the heads of the stairs; and in the evening the aisles would be crowded, above and below.

Immediately after his settlement, Mr. Ballou preached a sermon from 2 Thess. i. 7-9: "And to you who are troubled, rest with us, when the Lord Jesus shall be revealed from heaven with his mighty angels, in flaming fire, taking vengeance on them that know not God, and that obey not the gospel of our Lord Jesus Christ: who shall be punished with everlasting destruction from the presence of the Lord, and from the glory of his power." He attacked, with great force, the common doctrine of a general judgment, in the future state, for the actions of this life; and showed that his text gave no support to it. This sermon was published by Henry Bowen, and roused the indignation of Rev. Timothy Merritt, one of the Methodist clergymen of the town, who came out with an octavo pamphlet, entitled, "Strictures on Mr. Ballou's Sermon," &c. Mr. Ballou followed with a "Brief Reply" to the "Strictures"; and then came Mr. Merritt again, with "A Vindication of the Common Opinion relative to the Last Judgment and the End of the World, in Answer to Mr. Ballou's Reply." But the controversy did not end here. Mr. Ballou appeared with another pamphlet, entitled, "A Brief Reply to a Pamphlet entitled, 'A Vindication of the Common Opinion relative to the Last Judgment and the End of the World, in Answer to Mr. Ballou's Reply.'" Here the matter ended; and, whatever Mr. Merritt and his friends may have thought, the effect of the controversy was decidedly favorable to the rising popularity of Universalism.

For the last six or eight years preceding the rise of the Second Universalist Society, Universalism had produced little or no excitement in Boston. The First Society remained stationary. Mr. Dean, its pastor, preached little on those subjects on which he differed from other sects. In the vicinity of Boston there was no movement in favor of Universalism. There were scarcely ten Universalist pastors in Massachusetts. The cause was evidently languid.

The rise of the Second Universalist Society in Boston, and the removal of Mr. Ballou thither, produced a new state of things. There arose a commotion among the elements; but the effect was to purify the atmosphere, and give men a clearer and more extended vision. New Societies, holding Mr. Ballou's sentiments, soon began to arise around Boston; among which may be named the Societies in Roxbury and Cambridgeport. There was evidently a movement over the eastern part of the State, and adjacent States. The Society in Milford, Mass., erected an elegant house of worship, which was dedicated in January, 1821. A Society was formed in Providence, R. I., which built a splendid temple; and a meeting-house was also erected in Portland, Me. The people from Cape Cod frequently were in Boston on Sabbath days, and many of them attended on Mr. Ballou's preaching. They carried the seeds of truth into that section of the State, and societies sprung up in Barnstable, Brewster, Plymouth, &c., &c.

In 1821, the fact was announced (and it was very remarkable for that day), that there were twenty-three Universalist societies in Massachusetts. We scarcely know where that number could have been found at that time. To the best of our recollection, there were two societies in Boston, two in Gloucester, and one each in the towns of Charlestown, Salem,

Roxbury, Cambridgeport, Scituate, Shirley, Attleboro, Canton and Stoughton (one society for both), Marlborough, Milford, Oxford, Brookfield, Hardwick, and Dana. Some of these were small. We do not attribute to Mr. Ballou the rise of all the societies named; but it cannot be denied that his labors gave a new impulse to Universalism in Massachusetts.

Mr. Ballou preached many other sermons that were published, and especially a series entitled "Lecture Sermons," consisting of twenty-six, delivered on alternate Sabbath evenings, in the course of the year, between the months of July, 1818, and July, 1819. There were also other sermons published, preached by him which were subsequently collected into a volume, under the title of *Select Sermons*. In these two volumes Mr. Ballou's opinions are plainly stated, and logically defended. He shows, with great clearness, that the passages of Scripture generally used to sustain the doctrine of a judgment in the future state have no rightful reference to such a subject, but are applicable only to the things of time.

Mr. Ballou remained the sole pastor of this society for about twenty-five years, when it became the mutual wish of him and the people that he should be released somewhat from the cares that had laid upon him. A colleague was obtained; and, since that event, he has been at liberty to travel, as his inclination permitted. He has visited several of the States, attended many meetings of associations and conventions, and preached the gospel in a great number of places. He is now almost as able to preach as he ever was; and he is listened to, not for what he was, but for what he is. Seldom, very seldom, do we see a clergyman, so nearly four-score years of age, who has the strength of body and vigor of mind that Father Ballou possesses. We cannot look into the future; but, if we may judge from his present health and strength, we should not be astonished if he should live, and continue his public labors, for ten years to come.

> Hosea Ballou died a year and a half after this brief biography was published. In the four-volume *Life of Rev. Hosea Ballou*, Thomas Whittemore described Ballou's death as follows [pp. 296-298]:

On Sunday, the day before his death, he had restless sleep. He awoke as from a dream, and seemed very much fatigued. In his dream, he had been at a convention; he had had much to engage his attention; had been on several committees, seeking the prosperity and happiness of the religious order to which he belonged. He grew no better—rather worse; but still he complained not. He was, as we have said, always prepared to die. He had long contemplated his dissolution; and often said to his family that, at his age, his hold upon life must be very slender; and that, as he was so much away from home, they must realize that he might not be with them when he died. He was not only ready, but he was resigned, he was happy.

Said his daughter, Mrs. Wing (in whose family he died): "My father was perfectly calm, perfectly resigned. During his sickness, I sat up one night all alone with him; I wished to do it; I desired to have no one with me—it was a luxury to me to be with him through that night. He was so calm, so pleasant, so happy, that I felt calm, and almost happy myself, for I could not feel otherwise. It was good to be there; I could not bear to be interrupted." The end of that man was "peace."

Such, in brief, was the last sickness of father Ballou. ...

On Monday, 7th of June, he was evidently worse. All felt that he was *very* dangerously sick. His friend, Dr. A. R. Thompson of Charlestown called to see him. The hand of death, although the family knew it not, was then on him. He was about to be released. In parting with him, Dr. Thompson made some remark which the failing ear of the dying man did not distinctly catch; and, a moment afterwards, seeming to arouse a little, he uttered the words, "I do not think I *understood* what the doctor said." These were the last words he ever spoke. That eminent trait of his mind we see here active to the last,— a desire to *understand* everything to which his attention was drawn.

[Hosea Ballou died that same day, June 7, 1852. —Editor.]

SCRIPTURE INDEX

This index includes Ballou's citations or quotations of the Bible. Books are listed in the order they would have appeared in the Bible that Ballou used (i.e., the Protestant Christian Bible). Books that Ballou does not cite are also listed as a study aid for the reader.

Hebrew Bible

Genesis
 ii. 17, 54
 iii. 15, 43
 xii. 1-3, 166-167
 xii. 15-18
 xvii. 7-8, 129
 xvii. 13, 129
 xvii. 13-14, 167
 xxvi. 3-4, 167
 xlv. 5, 20
 xlviii. 3-4, 130
 xlviii. 26, 130
 xlix. 10, 169

Exodus
 xxii. 29, 178
 xl. 15, 130

Leviticus
 xvi. 34, 130
 xxvi. 44-45, 75

Numbers
 xv. 19-20, 178
 xviii. 15, 178
 xx. 27, 22

Deuteronomy

Joshua

Judges
 ix. 8-15, 155

Ruth

1 Samuel

2 Samuel

1 Kings

2 Kings

1 Chronicles

2 Chronicles

Ezra

Nehemiah

Esther

Job
 xxii. 5, 18

Psalms
 ii. 7-8, 171
 ii. 8, 102
 xiv. 2-3, 93
 xix. 11, 194
 xxii. 27, 171
 xxxiv. 8, 41
 xxxvii. 10, 170
 xxxvii. 36, 170
 xlv. 6, 101
 xlv. 7, 100, 101
 lxxii. 1, 169
 lxxii. 7-8, 169
 lxxii. 11, 169, 170
 lxxii. 17, 169
 xcvii. 7, 23
 cxviii. 26, 161

Proverbs
   iv. 18, 200
   vi. 19, 201
   vii. 23, 51
   xviii. 14, 51
   ix. 1-2, 194

Ecclesiastes

Song of Solomon
   ii. 11-12, 117
   v. 10, 94
   v. 16, 94

Isaiah
   iv. 4, 149
   ix. 6-7, 105
   ix. 19, 148
   xiv. 25, 75
   xxiv. 12, 26
   xxv. 6-8, 171-172
   xxvii. 9, 149
   xxxv. 10, 177
   xlv. 22-25, 184-185
   xlix. 6, 173
   xlix. 8, 173
   liii. 5-6, 70
   liii. 11, 188
   lxv. 5, 48

Jeremiah
   xxxiii. 20, 173

Lamentations

Ezekiel
   xviii. 20, 57
   xviii. 22-24, 173-174
   xxi. 30-32, 148
   xxii. 18-22, 148

Daniel
   vii. 14, 102, 173
   ix. 26, 138
   xii. 11, 139

Hosea

Joel

Amos

Obadiah

Jonah
   ii. 6, 131

Micah

Nahum

Habakkuk

Zephaniah

Haggai

Zechariah

Malachi
   iii. 1-3, 148-149
   iv. 1, 131, 132

New Testament

Matthew
   iii. 10, 131, 146
   iii. 10-12, 149
   iii. 12, 131, 146, 147
   iv. 5-6, 43
   v. 6, 195
   v. 13, 199
   v. 29-30, 131, 146
   v. 30, 147
   vii. 13-14, 131-132
   x. 12-15, 145
   x. 23, 135, 140, 143
   x. 27, 103
   x. 40-42, 145
   xi. 27, 102
   xi. 28-30, 191
   xi. 29, 199
   xii. 25, 152
   xii. 31, 19
   xii. 31-32, 156

SCRIPTURE INDEX

Matthew, cont.
  xiii. 30, 132, 146, 147
  xiii. 32-39, 136
  xiii. 40-42, 134-135, 147
  xv (entire), 132
  xvi. 27-28, 133
  xvi. 28, 140
  xvii. 12-13, 132-133
  xx. 1-16, 193
  xx. 12, 48
  xx. 24, 147
  xx. 37-39, 22
  xxi. 9, 161
  xxi. 31, 153
  xxi. 43, 153
  xxiii. 36, 140
  xxiv. 1-2, 136
  xxiv. 6, 137
  xxiv. 13-14, 137
  xxiv. 15-21, 138
  xxiv. 23, 136-137
  xxiv. 30-35, 140
  xxiv. 34, 140
  xxiv. 34-34, 142-143
  xxiv. 36, 100, 141, 142
  xxiv. 44, 142
  xxiv. 50, 142
  xxv. 1, 142
  xxv. 32, 143-144
  xxvii. 18, 102
  xxviii. 20, 201

Mark
  viii. 38, 133
  ix. 1, 134, 140
  xiii. 32, 100

Luke
  v. 30 ff., 193
  ix. 26-27, 134
  ix. 27, 140
  x. 27, 22
  xi. 9, 195
  xiv. 26, 152
  xv. 11-32, 193
  xvi. 19-31, 149-150
  xvi. 25, 153
  xvi. 31, 132

  xxi. 28-32, 135
  xxi. 32, 140
  xxi. 49, 189

John
  iii. 16, 91
  iii. 17, 91
  iv. 23-24, 48
  v. 19, 100
  v. 22-23, 184
  v. 39, 199
  vi. 53, 109
  vi. 63, 109
  viii. 44, 43
  x. 35, 25
  xii. 37-41, 154-155
  xiv. 6, 103
  xvii. 11, 101
  xvii. 18, 102

Acts
  iv. 27-28, 55
  xii. 45-47, 153
  xiii. 30-33, 166
  xiii. 32-33, 168
  xx. 35, 40
  xxvi. 23, 178

Romans
  iii. 13-18, 93
  iii. 19, 93
  iv. 21, 168
  v. 8, 92
  v. 11, 97
  v. 12, 93
  v. 22-23, 185
  vi. 1, 56
  vii. 19-23, 30
  vii. 23, 81, 107, 198
  viii. 1-2, 30-31
  viii. 2, 107
  viii. 3, 81
  viii. 6, 81, 82, 109
  viii. 20, 29
  ix. 16, 178
  ix. 21, 178
  ix. 21-22, 73-74
  xi. 7-10, 74, 153

Romans, cont.
 xi. 11-12, 74, 154
 xi. 15, 74, 154
 xi. 24, 75
 xi. 25-26, 75, 154

1 Corinthians
 iii. 3, 30
 x. 11, 147
 xv. 20, 178
 xv. 21, 179
 xv. 22, 179
 xv. 23-25, 180
 xv. 24-28, 13
 xv. 28, 181-182
 xv. 45, 31
 xv. 47-49, 182-183
 xv. 51-54, 183
 xv. 54, 172
 xv. 55, 155, 183
 xv. 56-57, 155

2 Corinthians
 v. 14-15, 185-186
 vi. 2, 194
 x. 4, 199

Galatians
 iii. 8, 168
 iii. 16-18, 165
 v. 17, 43
 v. 19-21, 30, 45

Ephesians
 i. 9, 175
 i. 9-10, 168-169
 i. 10, 169, 175
 i. 11, 176
 iii. 8, 198
 iv. 3, 201

Philippians
 ii. 9, 101
 ii. 9-11, 184
 iii. 21, 183-184

Colossians
 i. 19, 171

 i. 19-20, 188
 i. 20, 105, 168
 i. 21-22, 168

1 Thessalonians

2 Thessalonians
 1. 7-9, 132
 i. 7-10, 146
 i. 9, 147

1 Timothy
 i. 15, 198
 ii. 4, 174
 ii. 5, 103
 ii. 5-6, 70, 177

2 Timothy
 ii. 13, 37

Titus

Philemon

Hebrews
 i. 3, 31
 i. 6, 23
 i. 16, 25
 ii. 9, 70
 v. 2, 48
 vi. 17-20, 165-166
 vii. 11-12, 130-131
 viii. 6-8, 130
 viii. 10, 130
 ix. 26, 147
 xiii. 1, 200

James
 i. 14, 43
 i. 14-15, 31
 i. 15, 43
 i. 17, 60
 ii 26, 8
 iv. 1, 49

1 Peter

SCRIPTURE INDEX

2 Peter
   iii. 8, 53, 54
   iii. 9, 175

1 John
   ii. 1-2, 70
   iii. 17, 50
   iv. 8, 41
   iv. 9, 92
   iv. 10, 92
   iv. 16, 82, 82n.
   iv. 19, 41, 92
   iv. 20, 50
   v. 16, 19

2 John

3 John

Jude
   i. 3, 199

Revelation
   iii. 12, 100
   iii. 14, 100
   v. 9, 56
   v. 11-14, 180
   xiv. 10-11, 124
   xx. 17, 195
   xxi. 4, 172

GENERAL INDEX

This General Index is designed for the general reader, and for preachers and teachers, who are looking for persons and places, illustrations, and theological topics.

Ballou's vivid parables and illustrations are marked with an *asterisk.

---

*A who owes B 1,000 pounds, 66
Abraham, father of Israel, 20, 129, 165 ff., 189
    bosom of, 149 ff.
Adam, 12, 31 ff., 46, 63, 64, 65, 119
    death of, 33, 53
    as earthly nature, 179 ff., 197
    family, progeny or race of, 68, 76, 117, 151
    as heavenly, 203
    as moral agent, 84
    transgression of, 84-85
    unreconciled to Go, 90-91
Alexander, 43
*Algerian Dey enslaving five hundred Americans, 83-84, 177
*alphabet miserable except the vowel letters, 175-176
*American man and the lady with a sick father, 39-40
Antichrist, 125
*astronomers and the fly, 98-99
atonement
    was the effect (not cause) of God's love to humankind, 91 ff.
    erroneous theories of, 63-89
    erroneous system of, 75-79
    nature of, 108-120
angels, 24 ff., 43, 89, 125
    and Jesus, 133 ff., 140, 144 ff.
    in Revelation, 181
    Satan as an, 24 ff., 33-34, 42
autumn, 117

Babylon, King of, 26
beast (of Rev. xiv. 10-11), 124-125
Beezlebub, 151
*beggar and covetous man, 39
Bethlehem, 170, 187
Bible, 7-8, 48, 71, 119

Cain, 45
Canaan, 129-130
carnal mind, 48-49, 94, 109-112, 197 ff.
    in enmity against God, 42
    and Herod, 170
    and idolatry, 45
    overcoming, 81-82
    whether doctrine of Universalism is pleasing to, 191
    see also: Kings of the earth
cherubim, 32, 51, 111
*child and loaded pistol, 88
Christ, see: Jesus Christ
class (i.e., socioeconomic) bias, 190-191
conversion, not necessary for salvation, 113
covenant, 26, 75, 96-97, 110, 165, 175
    of circumcision, 129-130
    of flesh and spirit, 60

Daniel, 138-139, 200
David, 169, 171
Day of Judgment, 133, 145
denominations (of Christians), 46, 110
    objections to Universalism by other, 129-157
despair, at the thought of eternal punishment, 111, 114
devil, the, 33, 42-43, 46, 69, 79, 114, 151-152, 197
    existence of refuted, 42, 69
    see also: Satan
Diana (the goddess), 42
disputes, among Christians and

GENERAL INDEX 217

nations, 46
*drunkard and virtuous husband at an inn, 37-38

*earth in time of drought, 116
Elijah, 132-133
Eve, 31 ff.
evil
    existence of evil, 21-22
    moral evil, 28
    origin of natural evil, 28 ff.
Eden, Garden of, 31 ff., 90 ff.
    as figurative, 31-32
Egypt (of the Bible), 56, 68
England, 49
*Ezekiel in the holy waters, 202

*farm with a mortgage five times its value, 72
fire, 112, 131-132, 146-149, 189
    at the end of the world, 134-135
    sacred fire of love, 192
fire and brimstone, 111
    misinterpretation of in Revelation, 110-11, 124-125
France, 49
free will, 32-33, 34-37, 127-128
    can humans effect complete reconciliation in themselves, 104
fig-tree, 140, 155
    *soul as a, 116-117

God, 76-79
    as being of infinite perfection, 28
    as infinitely glorious, 76-77
    as infinitely good, 158
    is love, 41, 82
    loves humankind infinitely, 95
    loves humankind unchangeably, 91-92
    as shepherd, 196
    as Sun of righteousness, 117
    as Supreme Legislator, 15 ff.
    not a tyrant, 72 ff.
    seven spirits of, 99
    as unalterable, 97-98

    vengeance of, a false doctrine, 111
    wipes tears away from eyes, 172
government (divine), 79-80, 105, 163
government (human or earthly), 39
    of the mind, 196
    moral government, 104, 121
    needed due to sin, 50
grace, atoning, 58, 119-120
    efficacy of, 115
    like water in parched ground, 116-117

heaven, 32, 180-184, 190
    as duty, 195
    and Lucifer, 23 ff.
    not a place where the torment of others gives pleasure, 161 ff.
hell, 113, 114, 120, 122, 131, 136, 146
    of moral death, 50
    rich man in, 150 ff.
Herod, 55-56, 170
humankind, see: man

intention, and evil, 3, 20 ff.
idolatry, 45-46
Israel, 22, 135, 147, 152 ff., 156

Jacob's ladder, 197
jealousy, as a sin, 45
Jerusalem, 26, 56, 161
    destruction of, 143, 145 ff.
Jesus Christ
    causes humans to love holiness and hate sin, 108
    coming of Christ, 133 ff.
    consequences of the death of are good, 55
    a created dependent being, 100 ff.
    died for humankind, 70 ff.
    as heave offering, 178-179
    as image of God, 103
    as the Lamb, 125, 181
    as Mediator, 92, 100-106
    the power and kingdom of, 105
    he reveals God to sinners, 108
    resurrection of, 178-179

as second Adam, 31, 110, 189
sentient existence of, 12
suffering of, 82-84
Jewish nation
   "people of Israel," 55
   God's covenant with, 155, 165
Jews, 143, 145
   apostasy of, 109
   despising Christianity, 9, 191
   and Gentiles, 187
   and ignorance of Christianity, 22
   Jesus's war on, 135 ff.
   as "stars of God," 26
Job, 18
John the Baptist, 133
Joseph, 19-21, 54-56, 68
Judaism, as succeeded by Christianity, 154
Judas, 43
judgment, see: Day of Judgment

*Kings of the earth and the carnal mind, 170

law
   given to Israel, 22
   of God, 79-82
   and love, 108 ff.
law work vs. false education, 111-115
Lazarus and the rich man, 149-156
legislature, 15 ff., 79-80
   see also: Sate Legislature
liberty of will, see: free will
limitarians (those not believing in universal salvation)
   axiom thereof that God is not all mercy, 125
   mistaken views of, 74 ff., 175, 187
   plan of redemption of, 63-64
   proposition thereof that God consults the greatest good, 121-122
   supposition thereof that there is no alteration for the better after death, 126

love
   brotherly, 200-201
   and Christ, 185
   and damnation, 162
   and God, 182
   of God, 22, 40-41
   as God's moral law, 82
   as happifying, 42
   one thing needful for Christians, 118
   only thing that can do away with sin, 109-110
   stronger than death, 110
Lucifer, 23 ff.

man (humankind), 96
   all are endlessly miserable if one is, 160 ff.
   as both flesh and spirit, 30-31
   constituted to enjoy happiness, 158-159
   happiness the object of, 163-164
   as moral beings, 160-165
   original constitution of, 58-59
   unreconciled to Go, 94
*mankind like streams and rivulets running through the hill-country, 164
Milton, John, 24
money, love of, 49-50
Moses, 108, 115
*mother who could modify the desires of her child, 159

*neighbor who owes me a debt of 100 pounds, 65

*orange (fruit), loving it not because it is agreeable, 40-41

parables of Jesus, 7
   fig-tree, 135, 140
   prodigal son, 123, 193
   laborers in the vineyard, 119
   Lazarus and the rich man, 149-156
   sheep and goats, 143-144
   talents, 141-143

GENERAL INDEX 219

of the tares, 134-135, 147
ten virgins, 141-143
*Paradise Lost, retelling of, 23-28
*parent with ten children but provisions enough for only five, 122-125
*parent attending a child during an amputation, 162-163
Paul (Saul) of Tarsus, 56, 70, 97, 191, 199
   on the nature of Christ, 102 ff.
   a supporter of universalism, 73 ff., 174 ff.
*person invited by two friends, 34-35
*persons lost in the wood, 68-69
Peter, 43, 175, 201, 202
Pharisee, 108, 119, 136, 141, 157, 191, 193
   who feels as if something were coming to him, 197
*pineapple, argument about the taste of, 115-116
Pontius Pilate, 55-56
*poor man and the dollar or the guinea, 35-36
*poor man offered a thousand pounds for a day's labor, 194
predestination, 74, 175-177
*President of U.S. executed instead of seditious person, 668
pride, as a sin, 24, 48, 96, 197
*prodigal son and rich parent, 87
   see also: parables of Jesus

reason
   used to determine religious truth, 2, 27, 58, 68 ff., 113 ff.
   used to interpret scripture, 28
religion
   founded on human invention, 47
Restorationist controversy, alluded to, 6-7, 197, 200

Sabbath, 139
salt, 2, 199
salvation, 158-203

   from carnal mindedness, 192
   dependent on God, 173
   dependent not on Gospel obedience, 176
   of the elect a false doctrine, 74 ff.
   not limited to Christians, 110
   is universal, 121-128
   transcendent beauties of, 189
Satan, 26 ff., 151 ff.
   not author of sin, 33-34
   as a serpent, 42 ff., 189, 197
serpent, 24, 31 ff., 91, 110
   figuratively as false religion, 48
   as Satan, 42 ff., 189, 197
*serpent and child with loaded pistol, 88
shepherd who gives up large number of lambs to a wolf, 125-126
sin
   advantage of, 54
   as finite, 1-2, 15-19
   nature of, 15-22
   origins of, 23-44
   its torment-giving nature, 52
Solomon, 169
*spring (the season) is like faith in universal salvation, 117
*State Legislature, a resolve brought into, 16
*streams and rivulets reaching the ocean are like universal salvation, 164-165

Temple (of Jerusalem), 141
   destruction thereof, 137-139
   Jesus in the, 136-137
*thief who dares not steal, 52
*traveler, thirsting in the sands of Arabia, 41
*trees after autumn with faith in spring, 117
trinity, doctrine of
   logical inconsistencies in, 85-86, 101-103
   and payment of infinite debt, 65

unitarianism (the doctrine that

Christ is not God), 85-86, 100 ff., 107
universalism (the doctrine of universal salvation), 8, 127, 165
   converts to, 202
   knowledge of is progressive, 189 ff.
   leads us to knowledge of God, 193-194
   opens us to divine beauties, 188-189
   supposedly leads to wickedness, 118-119, 192

Universalists (believers in universal salvation), 195-196
   not heretics or infidels, 187
   misrepresentations of, 4-5
   more attentive to religious duties, 194
   some were formerly against the doctrine, 201-202

Washington, George, 177
will, see: free will
winter, 117, 138-139
world, the end of, 137 ff.

Other titles by Fish Island Books

LIBERAL PILGRIMS: VARIETIES OF LIBERAL RELIGIOUS EXPERIENCE IN NEW BEDFORD, MASSACHUSETTS

Unitarians, Universalists, and other religious liberals in New Bedford, Massachusetts. Essays on: Rev. William Jackson, the first African American minister to declare himself a Unitarians (in 1860); Mary Rotch, a primary influence on Ralph Waldo Emerson and theologian in her own right; Tryworks Coffeehouse, an outreach program to teens; and more.

428 pages. 2009.

UNITARIANS IN PALO ALTO, 1891-1934

A history of early Unitarianism in Palo Alto, California, told through the stories of individual Unitarians and Universalists, rather than through the stories of (mostly male) ministers. Includes extended biographical essays on Leila Lasley Thompson, war widow and Unitarian minister; Sylvie Thompson Thygeson, early provider of birth control; and Alice Locke Park, suffragist and pacifist; and more.

Forthcoming.

www.ingramcontent.com/pod-product-compliance
Lightning Source LLC
Chambersburg PA
CBHW031141160426
43193CB00008B/212